— By Lama Tendar & Ani Dechen —
BUDDHISM
The Science of Peace & Happiness

BUDDHISM
The Science of Peace & Happiness

Copyright © 2024 Lama Tendar and Ani Dechen

All rights reserved. Other than for personal use, no part of these cards or this book may be reproduced in any way, in whole or part, without the written consent of the copyright holder or publisher. These cards are intended for spiritual and emotional guidance only. They are not intended to replace medical assistance or treatment. The views and opinions expressed by the author, both within and outside of this publication, do not necessarily reflect the views of the publisher.

Published by Blue Gaia World Publishers©
80 Glen Tower Drive, Glen Waverley,
Victoria, Australia 3150

info@bluegaiapublishing.com
www.bluegaiapublishing.com

Edited by Jules Sutherland and Peter Loupelis
Designed by Sunshine Connelly

Blue Gaia World Publishers© is a registered trademark of Namaste Publishers Pty Ltd (ACN: 613 264 476), and part of the Blue Angel Publishing Group.

ISBN: 978-1-922574-02-2

BUDDHISM
The Science of Peace & Happiness

Introduction — 6

Part I — Background Knowledge of Buddhist Teachings — 8
How to Attain True Happiness? — 9
How to Cultivate Enlightened Aspiration? — 15
How to Be Completely Free From Suffering? — 23
How to Purify Negative Karma? — 25
Virtuous and Non-Virtuous Paths — 28
The Effects of Karma — 29
Buddhist Mind Training — 32
An Introduction to Buddhist Literature — 36

Part II — How to Work with This Deck of Cards — 40
Compassion Mandala — 41
Generate Pure Space with the Compassion Mandala — 48
A Meditation on Loving Kindness and Compassion — 51
Generating Wisdom Insights with the Cards — 55
Ritual to Purify Negative Karma — 55

Part III — Card Messages — 58
1. Innocent Mind — 59
2. Love — 60
3. Manifestation — 61
4. Karma — 62

5. Prayers — 63
6. Virtue — 64
7. Dedication — 65
8. Specifics — 66
9. Impression — 67
10. Faults — 68
11. Observation — 69
12. The Self — 70
13. Happiness — 71
14. Past — 72
15. Planning — 73
16. The Present Moment — 74
17. Disturbance — 75
18. Motivation — 76
19. Compassion — 77
20. Humbleness — 78
21. Rejoicing — 79
22. Remorse — 80
23. Mental Afflictions — 81
24. Attachment — 82
25. Anger — 83
26. Lethargy — 84
27. Self-Consciousness — 85
28. Anxiety — 86
29. Social Pressure — 87
30. Loss — 88
31. Limitation — 89
32. Expectation — 90
33. Time to Put Yourself First? — 91
34. Regeneration — 92
35. Guilt — 93
36. Actions — 94
37. Karmic Effects — 95
38. Equanimity — 96
39. Three Jewels — 97
40. Mother Sentient Beings — 98
41. Gratitude — 99
42. Appreciation — 100
43. Respect — 101
44. Creation — 102
45. Dissolution — 103
46. Generosity — 104
47. Trust — 105
48. Forgiveness — 106
49. Enlightened Aspiration — 107
50. Empowerment — 108
51. Mentality — 109
52. Transformation — 110

Glossary of Terms — 112
Appendix — 123
References — 123
Compassion Mantra — 124
Great Compassion Mantra — 124
About Lama Tendar — 126
About Ani Dechen — 127

INTRODUCTION

The Story Behind This Deck

Venerable Lama Tendar is a highly qualified and experienced spiritual teacher in Buddhism. He has been providing group and individual healing services in Australia for over 20 years. Since 2010, Lama Tendar has been running various healing courses, such as certified sound healing, mandala painting, and Medicine Buddha healing. Lama Tendar has also been providing authentic teaching and tailored guidance for advanced-level meditational practitioners who deeply appreciate the sincere care he extends to all his students.

Ani Dechen has been practising natural healing therapies for over 15 years and has been assisting Lama Tendar in teaching and preparing course materials for the past 10 years.

Upon the kind invitation from Toni Carmine Salerno, Lama Tendar and Ani Dechen have compiled into this deck of cards the advice based on Buddhist teachings that they have given to their clients and that they consider most helpful. They wish for this deck to be a good companion in your journey of developing a loving heart.

Through such efforts, they also wish to help generate good energy and a fulfilling mindset for anyone suffering from various mental conditions such as depression and anxiety, and to offer support to their family and friends.

Later in this guidebook, you will find longer messages that further elaborate on the short guidance on each card. In this introduction, suggestions are provided for how to work with the cards. Furthermore, this guidebook aims to provide relevant background knowledge on Buddhist teachings that can offer you wisdom and protection as you grow stronger spiritually.

May you enjoy a fulfilling life!

PART I

BACKGROUND KNOWLEDGE OF BUDDHIST TEACHINGS

Buddhist teachings offer a precise science in how to be free from the suffering of ageing, physical and mental sickness, and death — and to attain the true happiness of full enlightenment. This is a science because it is knowledge based on evidence. It is precise because it is founded on methods of specific reasoning, using accurate and comprehensive observations of the mind and its creations.

How to Attain True Happiness?

Buddha taught that, for all sentient beings to attain true happiness, the first step is the correct observation of suffering and its cause.

Feelings of physical and mental pain are easily observed and are typically what we identify as suffering. Physical and mental feelings of ease, on the other hand, are what we identify as happiness. Most of our daily efforts in pursuing happiness are devoted to acquiring what brings us this sense of ease.

Buddha, however, taught that this feeling of ease comes from the relief of painful feelings and thus is conditioned, rather than true, happiness. For example, sitting brings a feeling of ease on the legs if one has been on their feet for a long time. It is conditioned instead of true happiness due to the fact that sitting becomes suffering if one has been sitting for a long time. Putting all our efforts into acquiring what brings a sense of mental and physical ease is, therefore, effort in vain in terms of attaining true happiness.

Buddha taught that to experience true happiness, one needs to attain a body and mind that do not suffer — that is, a Buddha's body. The body of a sentient being, such as a human or an animal, is prone to ageing, sickness in body and mind, and death.

What determines, then, the type of body a sentient being is born into? It is karma. Karma is action — mental, verbal or physical. An action is bound to generate effects for the actor to experience in a future time. It is thus very important to be clear about the effects of our actions. We should thoroughly investigate this through our own experience and by observing the experience of others. For example, if someone performs a specific weight exercise for 10 minutes every day and eats protein-rich food, in three or so months, particular muscles will become obviously stronger. If we observe closely, it is the case that every move during the exercise sessions count. If the person exercises one side more than the other, an imbalance in muscle on the two sides of the body will also show up in due course.

Similarly, if we say something pleasant or unpleasant to a friend, we will get a different response. If we have been visualising an image during meditation, that image will appear easily in our mind.

After we have established, through thorough observation, that we are bound to experience the effects of every mental, verbal and physical action we have performed, it follows that there will be existence after we die from this life. Because it is not possible for us to have experienced the effects of every single action we have performed before our death—such as the thoughts generated in the mind or spoken the moment before death—we will be born again to experience the effects of past actions that we have not yet lived. What type of body we will be born into therefore depends on what actions we have performed in the past.

Buddha taught his disciples to observe the fact that virtuous actions bring future happiness and non-virtuous actions bring future suffering for the actor.

Virtuous and Non-Virtuous Actions

Virtuous actions are mental, verbal, and physical actions performed when at least one virtuous mental factor is present in the mind, such as compassion. Virtuous actions bring the performer favourable future conditions. They will find others more willing to offer them help.

Non-virtuous actions, on the other hand, are mental, verbal, and physical actions performed when non-virtuous mental factors are present in mind — for example, miserliness, anger, and jealousy. Such actions bring the performer unfavourable future conditions — more obstacles and less help. Being born into a body prone to suffering is therefore caused by non-virtuous actions one has performed in the past.

The root of all non-virtuous mental factors is ignorance of the nature of how all phenomena exist, especially the nature of how 'I' exist. This ignorance leads to an egocentric or selfish mentality. With this egocentric attitude, everything and everyone is perceived with a judgemental attitude according to whether or not 'this can benefit me'. Such a mentality easily gives rise to harmful actions towards others, and thus negative karma accumulates, leading to unfavourable rebirth.

The Nature of Mind

The opposite of the non-virtuous mind is the altruistic mind of a Buddha that perceives all sentient beings as being perfectly equal — all as dear as one's only child. This mentality of great compassion is founded on the wisdom of equanimity towards all sentient beings. Buddha sees equanimity in all sentient beings because Buddha's mind always abides in the natural state that transcends forms, thoughts, feelings, habits, and consciousness.

With such a perception, Buddha responds to the plea of each and every single sentient being in suffering with unconditional loving kindness and generosity. As a result, Buddha accumulates an immeasurable amount of merits that are the source of all happiness and attainments.

What, then, is this natural state of mind? The natural state of mind is like an open space with no edge and no centre, but with the potency to rise into any formation following any intent. This is the mind by itself. It is simultaneously and inseparably both knowing and brightness (energy). At this level, all phenomena are equal because they are all formations of the mind. This is the mind before any concepts are born or defined. This natural state of mind is the seed of Buddhahood in everyone. This is the Natural Truth Body of a Buddha.

This natural state of mind is pure and innocent and cannot be stained or marked permanently. To make a mark on the mind is like writing on water. The mark starts to disappear as soon as it is put on. Even deeper marks from repeated or habitual actions can disappear completely if the marking action is stopped. This is why habits can be changed.

Our mundane experience of the mind is endless thoughts and feelings. Thoughts and feelings, however, are not the mind. They are formations of the mind. Sentient beings are so absorbed in these thoughts and feelings that we cannot recognise the mind by itself. It is like we are constantly drawn into the emotional ups and downs of this movie and the next movie and have stopped noticing the fact that they are all films projected on a screen.

We are, thus, far removed from the reality of equanimity but constantly taking the side of this character and the next character in the illusional world of movies. Once we take a side, actions follow. We are then in conflict with other sentient beings who have assumed the sides of other characters in the movies. Negative karma thus accumulates, binding us all in the endless rebirth of suffering due to these actions.

Learning from Buddha's Example

How to be free from the control of negative karma then? We are fortunate to have the example of Shakyamuni Buddha to follow. Shakyamuni Buddha was a prince in India over 2500 years ago. He found a path out of the confusing illusions and the iron grip of negative karma, and reached full enlightenment.

In Mahayana teachings, Shakyamuni Buddha taught that to attain the ultimate happiness of full enlightenment, one must renounce the mundane intentions of acquiring only temporary happiness for oneself, and replace them with the intention of attaining full enlightenment for the benefit of all sentient beings. This enlightened aspiration—attaining full enlightenment for the benefit of all sentient beings—is the most important intention to cultivate for those seeking true happiness.

If, from now on, the only intention one ever had was purely to attain full enlightenment for the benefit of all sentient beings, then one would stop performing non-virtuous actions altogether and perform only virtuous actions. That means one would stop accumulating the causes to being born into a body prone to suffering, and would instead accumulate the causes to be born into the enlightened bodies of a Buddha. The non-virtuous actions that have already been done in the past would be purified so that the unfavourable conditions they would have brought in the future can be overcome. (More information on karma is presented later in this introduction.) How can a sentient being who is habituated to egocentric behaviour transform into one with altruistic motivation? The answer is as simple as sticking to the training. Because we experience the effects of every action we perform, whatever we practise, we get better at over time.

The good news is that we do not have to wait until we reach enlightenment to enjoy the benefits. Every action counts. Every time we perform an action with the enlightened motivation present in mind, we have created a cause for favourable conditions to rise sometime down the line. Life gets better and better if we persist in training ourselves to choose virtuous actions over non-virtuous ones for each matter at hand.

How to train in attaining enlightened aspiration? Shakyamuni Buddha left no less than 84,000 methods of training suitable for sentient beings with all types of mental dispositions. All these training methods eventually lead towards the ultimate happiness. A large volume of these methods are devoted to trainings in attaining enlightened aspiration. More discussion on this topic will follow in the next section.

The knowledge and practice of the path towards full enlightenment, and the end result attained, are the causes that give birth to the Wisdom Truth Body of a Buddha. The positive karma from the virtuous actions of working for the benefit of all sentient beings is the cause that gives birth to the form bodies of a Buddha — the Enjoyment Body, which is made of purified light that only beings with bodies made of light can see, and the Emanation Body, which can be seen by ordinary sentient beings like us. These three bodies, plus the Natural Truth Body mentioned before, are the four bodies of a fully enlightened Buddha.

Embodied with the full wisdom of perceiving reality, full knowledge of how to transcend root ignorance and all the suffering it causes, as well as merits vast as an ocean — a fully enlightened Buddha is thus always free from all types of suffering.

Mundane life intentions lead to birth into bodies prone to suffering, while altruistic intentions lead to birth into the perfect bodies of a Buddha, free from suffering. The way to attain true happiness, therefore, starts with establishing enlightened aspiration in one's mindstream.

How to Cultivate Enlightened Aspiration?

Buddhist mind training is not about getting the mind to do one thing or another. It is a journey with the clear aim of discovering true paths towards true happiness.

In the last section, we established the reasons, according to Mahayana teachings, why attaining full enlightenment is the way to attain ultimate happiness, and the key to moving towards this destination is generating enlightened aspiration. Mahayana teachings are suitable for those who are seeking not only their own relief but also the relief of many others from the suffering of ageing, sickness, and death.

In this section, we discuss the methods to cultivate the aspiration of attaining full enlightenment for the benefit of all sentient beings.

Small Steps

The correct method for generating such an aspiration is not to force the mind to renounce selfishness and to believe in enlightenment. Rather, it is a process of thoroughly investigating which of these two mentalities brings true benefits. It is a process with many steps before one's mind can operate spontaneously with the mentality of attaining full enlightenment.

At a coarse level, our mind is habituated with a self-centred mentality, constantly seeking more material wealth, praises, power, or social status, and sensual enjoyments for oneself and loved ones. However, deep down, we all have the Buddha seed — the natural state of mind. Therefore, even though we can't help to have selfish motivations, we truly admire altruistic behaviours. Our mind is softened when we are treated with great compassion.

The starting point is, therefore, just take a small step and give it a try. Try offering someone a small amount of help—within your capacity, without selfish reasons, but with a sincere good wish for the other person—and see; how does it feel for you?

If you are already doing this a lot and feeling the confidence of being a compassionate person, it is time to contemplate the correct reasons for cultivating enlightened aspiration and for renouncing a self-centred or self-grasping mentality.

Equanimity

First of all, enlightened aspiration is based on equanimity of all sentient beings; while the self-grasping mentality is based on the premise that oneself and one's loved ones are more important than others.

Here are some of the reasons that all sentient beings are equal:

- All sentient beings have the same natural state of mind that cannot be permanently stained.
- All sentient beings have the seed of compassion.
- All sentient beings enjoy happiness in terms of a mental and/or physical sense of ease.

- All sentient beings avoid suffering in terms of a mental and/or physical sense of pain.
- All sentient beings experience the effects of their virtuous and non-virtuous actions.

Therefore, there are good reasons for cultivating enlightened aspiration.

Compassion for All

Furthermore, if one, through thorough investigation, establishes that every action generates effects for the actor to experience in due course, then one must accept the position that there is an endless circling of birth, ageing, and death; because we could never finish experiencing the effects of all the past actions before the death of any lifetime. It follows that any sentient beings—even those we currently consider enemies—could have been our parents, siblings, children, best friends, and loved ones in a past lifetime. Those we love dearly this lifetime could be born as any sentient being after they pass away. Therefore, it does not make sense to exclude any sentient being from our loving kindness and compassion, even our enemies.

If we think, "There are so many people I never know and never have anything to do with. Why should I work for their benefit?" — think again. The clothes we are wearing, who transported them from the factory to the shops? Who made them? Who designed them? Who made the fabric used to make the clothing? Who planted the cotton used to make the clothing?

Apply this reasoning to all the good things we enjoy: housing, food, cars, etc. Behind each of these are people we think we will never know or have anything to do with. We might say that we paid money for these goods and services, but think — where does our money come from? It is through the kind patronage of clients and customers that we earn our money. Therefore, it makes sense to include all sentient beings in our loving kindness and compassion.

As a matter of fact, *every single day*, our very own life is saved — by our parents and carers when we are young and by those who make it possible for us to access food, clothing, housing, etc., after we grow up. It is only fair for us to devote all our life to working diligently for their benefit. What, then, do we work on for their benefit? What do they need?

Happiness for All

They need true happiness. They need true relief from the suffering of going uncontrollably through the endless circling of birth, ageing, sickness, and death. How can I help with this? How can I free them from the endless suffering of ageing, sickness, and death? *Only by attaining full enlightenment*. Only if I attain the fully enlightened state of a Buddha am I able to lead people on the correct path towards the true happiness of enlightenment. Therefore, I must firmly generate enlightened aspiration and work for the benefit of all sentient beings. This is the correct reason for generating enlightened aspiration. At this point, rest your mind in the virtuous state generated by this reasoning and enjoy the blissful blessing.

If you do such contemplation every day and practise loving kindness towards others as much as you can, your energy level will be elevated, and your heart will become more open and joyful. People will find your company more enjoyable. Most importantly, you will be accumulating more causes for future true happiness.

Doubts and Rejuvenation

Up to this stage, even if your mind has mostly accepted the position that enlightened aspiration is superior to the self-grasping mentality in terms of living a fulfilling life, you may still have doubts. For example, you may think, "I've been compassionate to everyone, and that makes me so tired. So I just want to think about myself now."

To fully develop an enlightened mind, one needs to thoroughly investigate these cases. Does being compassionate make one tired? The answer is no. Because working for selfish reasons can also make one tired. The direct cause of tiredness is not knowing when to rest and how to rejuvenate.

Shakyamuni Buddha became very powerful because he expanded his capacity to benefit all sentient beings. He matured from a prince to a fully enlightened Buddha. The whole idea of enlightened aspiration is to empower oneself, to increase one's own capacity so as to be able to bring all sentient beings to the state of full enlightenment.

As a matter of fact, when the mind is in a virtuous state, the wind energy in the body is positive and nurturing. So, contemplating enlightened aspiration itself is the most supreme source of good energy. One feels tired when the mind turns away from great compassion and falls back to the self-grasping mentality with negative images of one's own body. The correct attitude for rejuvenation comes from the enlightened intention of self-empowerment: "I must become healthier, physically and mentally, so that I can work properly for all sentient beings."

The difference is that, with the self-empowering attitude, the mind holds a positive image of oneself becoming healthier; with the self-pity attitude, the mind holds a negative image of one's own body full of pain and tiredness. With the mind itself being pure and innocent, whatever image we hold about ourselves, we will be shaped into it. That is why it is beneficial to visualise a virtuous image of a Buddha and contemplate the enlightened aspiration of a Buddha during meditation. This is an effective way to rejuvenate.

One might also doubt by thinking, "If I pay so much attention to others' wellbeing, and if I do not try to look after myself, how can I be happy? What about me?"

The answer is that with the self-centred mentality, one cannot fulfil the goal of bringing oneself happiness. The mundane objectives of happiness are to accumulate more material wealth and gain higher social status so that we can enjoy more pleasant things in life and thus be admired by others. Any actions driven by these mundane motivations are bound to attract more and more enemies through jealousy and conflicts of interest, and push away virtuous friends. With fewer and fewer opportunities to perform virtuous actions, our merits quickly run out, and thus we fall into misery.

On the contrary, with an aspiration to enlightenment, one is devoted to work for others' wellbeing. Actions driven by such pure motivation are bound to generate more and more virtuous friends and drive away non-virtuous ones. With more opportunities to perform virtuous actions, one's own future happiness is guaranteed. It is for the sake of each sentient being's very own wellbeing that Buddha recommended the path of working towards the enlightenment of all sentient beings as the way to generate true happiness.

Another doubtful attitude could be, "Enlightenment is wonderful, but that is so far-fetched compared to my humble goals in life. I never thought I could attain enlightenment." Here, the right question to ask is, "Have I managed to reach my humble goals of happiness in life?"

The answer is, of course, no. We want to be healthy, and sometimes we do manage to recover from illness. But another sickness soon hits. We seem to be forever trying to get out of one after another physical and mental conditions or trying not to fall into one after another such conditions. This is because our self-centred mentality determines that our efforts in attaining happiness will not be fruitful due to lack of merits, as discussed above.

The tremendous efforts required to fend off one suffering after another, if applied properly towards the right cause, could certainly bring us more happiness along the way, as we move closer to the ultimate happiness.

Happiness

If I only work for my own happiness, my happiness is easily disturbed when my parents and children are not happy. If I only work for the happiness of myself and my family, our happiness is easily disturbed if my child's best friend is not happy. Continue to apply such reasoning, and we reach the conclusion that even if there is one sentient being left unhappy, I cannot have true happiness. This is why the only way to attain stable happiness for oneself is to work for the true happiness of all sentient beings. This is why we must all attain enlightenment for us to have stable happiness.

Beyond Self-Grasping

After all the doubts are removed through thorough investigation, we reach a stage of conviction at the conceptual level for generating enlightened aspiration. However, we still have the old habit of applying the self-grasping mentality.

At this stage, more practice of compassionate action is important. We do this by assuming the enlightened aspiration as the virtuous motivation for daily life activities. For example, instead of thinking, "I have to work to make a living for myself and my family," we can think of our daily job as a wonderful opportunity to serve many others every day. With this attitude, the job becomes empowering and enjoyable. Instead of thinking, "I want to be healthy to avoid pain," we can think, "I want to maintain good health so that I can work to benefit those around me," or, "I want to keep my mental strength so that others can benefit from it."

The secret of keeping a healthy body and mind is this: whenever we are enjoying a pleasant experience, we can think, "May all sentient beings also have such joy." And whenever we have a painful experience, we can think, "May all sentient beings be free from such suffering." This way, the mind is always directed towards generating more happiness. Such actions are causes for more happiness in the future.

With such daily practices, one can gradually become familiar with acting upon enlightened aspiration. However, for the enlightened aspiration to rise spontaneously in one's mindstream, one needs to stabilise the enlightened aspiration in their mind through meditation. One should seek guidance from an authentic guru to develop such a meditation practice.

How to Be Completely Free From Suffering?

If you have developed some conviction about renouncing the self-grasping mentality and the resulting suffering of ageing, sickness, and death and have made some progress in cultivating enlightened aspiration, it is time to work on attaining the wisdom of emptiness. This wisdom is what severs us from the ignorance that is the root cause of all suffering. This wisdom cannot be attained without first broadening our perspective by cultivating enlightened aspiration.

Emptiness

What is emptiness? Emptiness is not nothingness. Emptiness is defined as 'free from inherent nature'. For example, a large dining table is not inherently a large dining table, because it can also be used as a large benchtop for artwork or even a nice bed in case of need. What it is depends on the specific situation. For example, on Christmas Day, when the whole family is home for lunch, it is a large dining table. During school holidays, it can be a large benchtop for the kids' artwork. If it is inherently a large dining table, then it can only be used as a large dining table and nothing else, which is obviously not true. The fact is that the large table in the dining room can be used for multiple purposes. Therefore, it is not inherently a dining table. Another good example is that a person does not have any inherent nature. If we say a person has the inherent quality of being angry, then we are saying that the person is angry at all times, in all locations, and towards all people. That is obviously not true. Even if someone yells angrily at least once a day, there is still the larger part of the day when they are not yelling angrily — when they are eating their favourite food or are in the company of their favourite person, for example.

It is unfounded to deduct from a few incidents of angry yelling that the person's nature is inherently angry. It is incorrect to judge someone as being always angry from specific incidents of angry outbursts. The reality is that the person is angry in certain situations, with particular causes and conditions.

Due to the nature of the mind, what made someone angry yesterday may not make them angry again today. We are good at changing our minds, however stubborn we might appear to be. Therefore, no one has the inherent nature of being angry, nor do they have any other inherent nature for the same reasons. In fact, we are forever evolving forwards and being shaped by our experiences. In other words, the mind can be trained to replace non-virtuous habits with virtuous habits. We are thus capable of attaining full enlightenment.

Emptiness is the true mode of existence of people and objects. Ignorance about this true mode of existence is the root cause of all suffering. If we judge from an angry outburst that a person is inherently angry, then we will assume a negative attitude towards this person and generate negative karma in relation to them. If we see an incident as an incident and treat the person with the loving kindness of understanding, we will generate positive karma.

Similarly, if we judge ourselves as being inherently incapable of being compassionate from one failed attempt to help others, we will never acquire that inner quality. If we see the failed attempt as one failed attempt, then we are open to further attempts in a more correct manner, which will eventually lead to an inner quality of fully developed compassion — enlightenment.

Fully developed compassion is supported by the wisdom of emptiness. If we perceive sentient beings as having an inherent nature, then sentient beings are not equal — those who are bad are forever bad, and thus we should always avoid them; those who are good are forever good, and thus, we should try to always stick to them. Without equanimity, extending loving kindness towards all beings is not possible. Only when we perceive incidents as incidents—and sentient beings as being free from inherent qualities and thus capable of changing their behaviour—can we attain an altruistic mind.

Therefore, emptiness means sentient beings and objects are empty of inherent nature. It does not mean that there are no sentient beings and/or there are no objects. It means the true mode of existence is that we are constantly evolving forwards, shaped by the actions we choose to perform moment by moment. It means if we habituate ourselves to choose to act in accordance with the enlightened aspiration, we have the flexibility to change and evolve into the perfection of full enlightenment.

How to Purify Negative Karma?

With the help of the correct perception of reality, we can make good progress in cultivating enlightened aspiration. This increases our chance of choosing virtuous actions for each matter at hand. However, what about the non-virtuous actions we have already performed in the past? They are manifesting now as obstacles and mental obstructions, making it difficult for us to enjoy the good fruits of our virtuous karma and to accomplish more virtuous deeds. They lead us down the wrong path — paths of suffering. How do we deal with them?

Negative karma can be purified by applying four powers:

1. The power of reliance
2. The power of confession
3. The power of turning away from faults
4. The power of applying remedies

The Power of Reliance

The first power involves relying on a strong, virtuous force for protection, for example, Buddhas and their offspring. Negative karma works by creating situations that we feel we have to respond to by choosing non-virtuous actions. We, therefore, need powerful help from a Buddha or a high-level practitioner of Buddhist teachings to show us how to break free from the illusion by pointing out the facts or where or how we have seen it wrongly.

The Power of Confession

The second power comes from revealing every single non-virtuous action we have performed, to the virtuous force we have chosen to rely on. The more we contemplate the negative effects of non-virtuous actions, the deeper our regret, and the more effective the purification action is. If, after we perform a non-virtuous action, we immediately regret it, the karmic effect of the non-virtuous action and its subsequent negative habits become weaker.

The Power of Turning Away from Faults

The third power requires the determination never to repeat the non-virtuous deeds ever again. The stronger the determination is, the more effective the purification is. With this determination, our mind becomes alert and adept at saying no to invitations to perform non-virtuous actions.

The Power of Applying Remedies

The fourth power involves performing virtuous actions so as to accumulate good karma. When negative karma matures, and its effects show up as unfavourable conditions, it is like a bad influence that leads us to perform more non-virtuous actions. When positive karma is accumulated through purification practice, a very strong positive influence will also show up — much stronger than the negative one. We can therefore accomplish our virtuous choice in the moment, despite the negative influence. In other words, the negative influence will be overcome so that we are protected from it. The positive force generated through proper purification is stronger — because the negative influence is founded on illusion, while the virtuous influence is based on facts.

Together, these four powers work to increase the chance of us making virtuous instead of non-virtuous choices. Thus, the way to purify negative karma is to prevent non-virtuous habits from leading us to perform more non-virtuous actions now and in the future.

So, what are virtuous and non-virtuous actions, and what kind of effects can they bring in the future?

Virtuous and Non-Virtuous Paths

Shakyamuni Buddha taught 10 paths of action, which are described in detail by Lama Tsong Khapa in Volume 1, Chapter 14 of *The Great Treatise on the Stages of the Path to Enlightenment*.

The 10 non-virtuous paths of action are:

- Three physical actions: killing, stealing, and sexual misconduct.
- Four verbal actions: lying, divisive speech, offensive speech, and senseless speech.
- Three mental actions: covetousness, malice, and wrong view.

The 10 paths of virtuous action involve correctly restraining from performing the 10 non-virtuous actions.

A path of action has four aspects:

- The basis
- The attitude that leads to motivation
- The implementation of the action
- The culmination of the action

For example, the basis for killing is that a sentient being is alive; the attitude is an afflictive mental factor—such as anger and strong attachment—leading to a motivation to kill; the implementation is the action of killing, either by doing it oneself or asking someone else to do it; the culmination is that the living being is no longer alive, due to the action.

The corresponding virtuous action is either to refrain from killing as described above, or to save a life. The virtuous action of saving a life is motivated by compassion, wishing the sentient being to be free from the suffering of sickness and death.

The fundamental difference between virtuous and non-virtuous paths of action starts with the motivation for the action. It is, therefore, crucial for those seeking happiness to become alert to what types of mental factors are present in their mind. Virtuous mental factors such as great loving kindness and compassion lead to virtuous motivation. Non-virtuous mental factors—such as ignorance, attachment, anger, pride, jealousy, and doubt—lead to non-virtuous motivation.

The Effects of Karma

The effects of karma are three-fold:

- Fruition effects
- Causally concordant effects
- Environmental effects

Taking, for example, the virtuous action of correctly saving a life or refraining from killing, the fruition effect is to be born into the god or human realms. The causally concordant effect is a healthy and long life span. The environmental effect is that food, drink, medicine, and fruit have potency and power, are easy to digest, and bring health.

The effects of negative karma are the opposite of those of positive karma. The law of karma means that one will definitely experience the effects of their karma unless their negative karma has been purified.

To most of us, the content of the law of karma itself is not unfamiliar: mental, verbal, and physical actions have an impact on the actor's future. Virtuous actions bring merits and happiness; non-virtuous ones bring suffering to the actor sometime down the line. However, applying this idea consistently in our decision-making is hard. It requires a more detailed knowledge of how the law of karma works. It also takes training to incorporate the understanding into our daily life activities.

The Continuum of Lifetimes

Most of us accept that 'practice brings improvement'. However, as soon as we spot that others seem to be better at a certain skill than we are, with less practice, we immediately give up the right idea and turn to the superstition that they are just naturally better or born better for no reason. Based on this superstition, we often give up our good efforts to achieve excellency.

The correct reasoning, consistent with 'practice brings improvement', as to why somebody is better at something than me is that they must have practised more than I am aware of, or they must have practised this skill in a past life or lives. Thus, a mind that subscribes consistently to 'practice brings improvement' should come to the conclusion that there are previous existences before this current life. Otherwise, we cannot explain why someone can, for example, play the piano beautifully at five years of age.

Similarly, most of us accept that 'actions bring consequences'. However, not many of us are keeping a strict practice of moral discipline and applying diligence in purifying our negative karma. Rather, we are getting comfortable with the attitude that says, "I do not want to hear about it," as if not hearing about it can stop us from experiencing the consequences. Based on this attitude, we let our moral standards degenerate and follow the bad example of those who maximise temporary benefits as if there is no tomorrow.

The correct reasoning for those who subscribe consistently to 'actions bring consequences' is that there are future lives after death, in which we experience the consequences that we do not experience this lifetime.

This view of a continuum of lifetimes is important because of its impact on our choice of actions. Without it, our choice of actions becomes rather short-sighted. If we limit our view to what happens within this one lifetime, we might witness those who are ethically wrong enjoying good material wealth while those who are ethically good suffer from material poverty. This can distract us from acting in line with the idea that 'actions bring consequences'.

Perceiving our own existence as a continuum of lifetimes offers a broadened view to support us in choosing virtuous actions that bring happiness. Under this broadened perspective, those who keep good ethical conduct and are suffering material poverty can be understood as having performed non-virtuous actions in past lives but are now correcting their behaviour for good. Those who appear to have low morals and are experiencing material wealth can be understood as having performed great virtuous deeds either in their past lives or in an unannounced way in this lifetime.

Most importantly, the view of life as a continuum of lifetimes encourages us to diligently accumulate merits. Under such a broadened perspective, the more virtuous and less non-virtuous deeds one performs, the brighter one's future and future lives are guaranteed to be.

Practice brings improvement. The good news from the law of karma is that we can all achieve enlightenment. All it takes is patience and perseverance in accumulating virtuous merits and wisdom insights. Every action counts. Even if one moves as slow as a snail, one will reach enlightenment as long as one is on the right path and heading in the right direction.

Due to our formation of the egocentric mentality, we are constantly accumulating negative karma. Therefore, just like we need to take a shower or brush our teeth every day, we also need to perform the purification of negative karma every day in order to enjoy a happier and happier life until we reach full enlightenment.

Try performing the beautiful ritual presented later in this guidebook every day (see 'Ritual to Purify Negative Karma'). Make it short and enjoyable. You will feel much younger and lighter, with less and less baggage of the past to carry.

Practice brings improvement. The more virtuous practices we introduce into our lives, the more we benefit from the natural law of karma. As the virtuous momentum gathers, the process of adopting the mentality of enlightened aspiration—the root cause of all happiness—also becomes easier.

Buddhist Mind Training

The realisation of emptiness requires prolonged observation, with a stable mind, of the nature of existence. Developing mental concentration is thus a necessary part of Buddhist mind training.

Buddhist teachings and practices form an effective path towards true happiness because they are founded on the comprehensive and precise knowledge of how the mind works. An in-depth understanding and map of the mind at work forms the basis of mind training. Buddhist mind training starts with the practice of developing alertness to one's own mental state and the mental factors at work. This awakening of the mind offers a foundation for renouncing non-virtuous mental habits that are the source cause of all suffering and replacing them with virtuous ones.

Coarse-Level Mind

The coarse-level mind is the one associated with the six sense powers — those of the eye, ear, nose, tongue, body, mental sense powers and respective sense consciousness. Our daily life and work activities, as well as thoughts and feelings, involve the function of the mind at this coarse level. The sixth or the 'mental' sense power and sense consciousness engaged at this level is the conceptual mind. The coarse-level mind rides on the coarse-level 'wind' or energy to contact its object of engagement. Raging anger never lasts too long because the person's energy is quickly exhausted. This is why someone might feel cold and depleted after a flare of anger.

Very Subtle Mind

Beyond the coarse level, there's the very subtle mind that transcends concepts. The very subtle mind is always accompanied by the very subtle wind. This inseparable pair lives in the depth of the centre of the heart chakra. This is the unceasing mind. To the very subtle mind, the very subtle wind is like its body. So technically, we can never die. What we define as death is actually the separation of the subtle-level existence (the very subtle mind and its accompanying very subtle wind) from the coarse-level body.

The real challenge is actually what kind of coarse-level existence is manifested. That is governed by the law of karma. Virtuous mental, verbal, and physical actions leave virtuous imprints in the subtle mind and result in a happy coarse-level existence; non-virtuous actions leave non-virtuous imprints at the subtle level and result in suffering at the coarse level.

The Six Realms of Existence

The six realms of existence are understood to be:

1. God realm
2. Demi-god realm
3. Human realm
4. Animal realm
5. Hungry ghost realm
6. Hell realm

Of the six realms, the human and god realms are considered to be the happier realms. The hell realm beings are totally controlled by the mental affliction of anger. The hungry ghost beings suffer the karma of miserliness. The animal realm beings suffer the karma of mental dullness. The demi-god realm beings suffer from fighting and quarrelling due to the karma of jealousy. The god realm beings suffer from declining power and status due to pride. The human realm is considered the existence with the best opportunities for attaining full enlightenment, especially if one has the leisure to study and practise wisdom teachings.

Within the six-realm existence, human beings are best positioned to accumulate positive karma for enlightenment. A meaningful human life thus means accumulating as many merits and wisdom insights as possible. To those who are inspired, the authors strongly recommend Buddhist mind training.

Given the innocent nature of the mind, the process of mental transformation for attaining happiness is nothing more than becoming familiar with the truth that enlightened aspiration leads to happiness. However, mental transformation involves many steps, according to the various types of cognition taught in Buddhist texts (an English translation is presented in *Mind in Tibetan Buddhism* by Lati Rinbochay and Elizabeth Napper). Therefore, it takes patience and perseverance to accomplish the transformation.

The Stages of Learning

When we first hear about something new and foreign, we often tend to dismiss it as being unimportant, feeling, "It's not for me."

After we have heard about it frequently enough and witnessed its good effects on others, our attitude can shift to, "Maybe it's something worthwhile trying." This shift in attitude leads to our investigation of the idea through experience. Because it's truth, the results of the investigation provide ample evidence that it is beneficial. This typically takes us to a position of thinking, "It's basically true, but I still have doubts about it."

At this stage, it's important that we persevere in our efforts by taking a closer look at the cases where the evidence appears to be negative. After clearing away our doubts, we reach a position where we are fully convinced at the conceptual level that compassion brings happiness.

However, our action is still habitually geared towards the wrong idea that being egocentric benefits us. This last hurdle can only be overcome with perseverance in meditation, single-pointedly focusing on truth until we *act spontaneously according to truth*. This step also involves consistency in choosing virtue while abandoning non-virtue in daily life.

To facilitate this process, we need to accumulate as many merits as we possibly can. Meditations on loving kindness and compassion and offering mandalas are beautiful ways to aid this.

An Introduction to Buddhist Literature

The Path to Enlightenment

The three key aspects of the path towards full enlightenment are:

1. Renouncing the repeated suffering of birth, ageing, sickness, and death

2. Generating enlightened aspiration

3. The wisdom of emptiness

This is succinctly summarised and clearly explained by Lama Tsong Khapa in his work titled *Three Principal Aspects of the Path*.

In his renowned work *The Great Treatise on the Stages of the Path to Enlightenment*, he presented detailed instructions on how to practise the path towards enlightenment for beings with small, medium, and large capacities. Beings with a small capacity are those who wish to be reborn into a better life within the circling of birth, ageing, and death. Beings with a medium capacity are those who wish to transcend this circling for themselves. Beings with a large capacity are those who are interested in finding ways to true happiness, not only for themselves but for many others as well.

As discussed earlier, generating enlightened aspiration is the key to getting on the right path for beings with a large capacity. To this end, Buddhist teachings present a very rich body of effective means for establishing enlightened motivation. Two examples of such works are Volume Two of Lama Tsong Khap's *The Great Treatise on the Stages of the Path to Enlightenment* and *Activating Bodhichitta and a Meditation on Compassion* by His Holiness, the XIV Dalai Lama. This fine body of literature demonstrates the reasoning why selfishness—including the self-grasping and self-cherishing mind—is based on misconceptions of reality and is the source of all suffering. It establishes through reasoning why great loving kindness and compassion are the right attitudes, which are founded on truth and lead to happiness. These works offer meditational methods to help one act according to the right view.

Furthermore, this body of literature includes a full range of detailed instructions for how to cultivate great compassion and behave correctly in a degenerated environment as we have. Among all the wonderful instructive writings, the one that a sincere practitioner must study is Master Shantideva's *A Guide to the Bodhisattva's Way of Life*.

Teachings on Emptiness

The third key aspect of the path towards enlightenment is the realisation of the wisdom of emptiness. The teachings presented in this guidebook are based on the Buddhist tenet '*Prasangika Madhyamaka*' (The Middle Way), which was established by Indian Master Nagarjuna in his work *Mulamadhyamakakarika*. In accordance with the prophecy of Shakyamuni Buddha, Nagarjuna elucidated the definitive meaning of emptiness through the reasoning known as 'dependent origination'.

'Dependent origination' is the idea that all phenomena exist dependent on causes and conditions, rather than existing independently. This goes hand in hand with the idea of emptiness — that all phenomena are free from any inherent nature. Because their existence depends on causes and conditions, they are subject to change, so they cannot exist inherently. Only if a person is free from any inherent qualities can the person change in response to virtuous or non-virtuous influences (causes and conditions).

The Nature of Existence

Master Nagarjuna's disciple Venerable Aryadeva, in his renowned work *Four Hundred Stanzas on the Middle Way*, offers step by step reasoning to clear all misconceptions about the nature of existence. The first eight chapters of the work refute, one by one, the misconceptions in our daily life and point out clearly how all negative emotions—such as anger, attachment, pride, and jealousy—are based on misconceptions of reality. The following eight chapters present a manual on how to refute all misconceptions about the nature of existence.

Lama Tsong Khapa, in his work *The Great Treatise on the Stages of the Path to Enlightenment*, also devoted Chapters 7–27 of Volume Three to the topic of the correct view of the nature of existence.

The Law of Karma

For those building happiness in life, an appreciation of the deeper meaning of the law of karma works as a solid foundation. The law of karma is a natural law that governs all creations, from ordinary people to fully enlightened beings. Its validity is founded on the nature of mind at the most profound level. Lama Tsong Khapa gives a precise and comprehensive explanation of the law of karma in *The Great Treatise on the Stages of the Path to Enlightenment* (Volume One, Chapters 13–15).

About the Mind

Master Kamalashila's work, *The Stages of Meditation*, offers instruction on how to focus the mind on the right object of meditation and how to develop mental concentration in gradual stages.

Buddhist teachings and practices offer insights into how to train the mind to replace non-virtuous habits with virtuous ones. *Mind in Tibetan Buddhism* by Lati Rinbochay and Elizabeth Napper offers an English translation of the Buddhist texts on the various types of mind and mental factors.

PART II

HOW TO WORK WITH THIS DECK OF CARDS

There are many ways to utilise this set of cards. You can draw a card for an occasional message. You can draw a number of cards in any layout to seek deeper insights into a situation. You can explore ways to develop inner qualities. You can also develop your meditation with the cards. Most importantly, we wish for the cards to help you grow stronger and stronger spiritually with a loving heart.

In this introduction on how to use the cards, we first introduce to you the Compassion Mandala featured on each of the cards. This is followed by some short rituals and meditations that are mind-training methods for developing loving kindness and compassion, as well as purifying negative karma.

Compassion Mandala

This Compassion Mandala was painted by Ani Dechen, from July 2009 to December 2010, under the guidance of her teacher, Lama Tendar. In Tibetan Buddhist traditions, mandalas created with sand or painted on paper originate from Shakyamuni Buddha's teaching. The details of the mandala—including its structure, colours, and symbols—are passed down through an unbroken verbal lineage from teachers to students. The creation of mandalas forms part of the Buddhist mind-training methods for cultivating inner qualities of wisdom and great compassion.

Avalokiteshvara — Buddha of Compassion

The Compassion Mandala represents the enlightened mind, body, and speech of Avalokiteshvara — the Buddha of Compassion. Avalokiteshvara is the name of the Buddha of Compassion in Sanskrit (in Chinese, it is Guanyin and Chenrenzi in Tibetan). Avalokiteshvara symbolises the essence of great compassion in all Buddhas and their offspring, the Bodhisattvas.

At the centre of the Compassion Mandala is a square palace with four doors. At the very centre of the palace, on top of the multicolour, eight-petal lotus, is Avalokiteshvara, whose symbol is the lotus, representing purity. The lotus grows out of mud, but its flower is completely pure.

In the Tibetan Buddhist tradition, Avalokiteshvara is visualised as having a white-coloured body, one face and four arms, sitting on a lotus and moon cushion. The first two hands hold a wish-fulfilling jewel in front of his heart, symbolising the fully enlightened state and, thus, the full capacity to help all sentient beings. The second right hand holds a string of mala beads, and the second left hand holds the stem of a lotus with the blossoms close to his left ear. His whole body emits five-coloured wisdom lights that are pure blessings for all sentient beings. We can engage Avalokiteshvara's help by calling his name or chanting the Compassion Mantra:

OM MANI PEME HUM

Avalokiteshvara also has a formation with 11 heads and 1000 arms (with an eye on each of the 1000 hands) standing on a lotus and moon cushion. This form illustrates his capacity as the all-seeing one, in possession of factual information in all directions and in all details. It also shows his capacity to deliver needed help to sentient beings effectively. Great compassion in its fully developed form is supported by a direct perception of the nature of existence and is thus detailed and precise.

The 1000-arm form symbolises that Avalokiteshvara has fulfilled his great vows — to instantaneously see any sentient being who is calling his name in need of urgent help, and to deliver the requested help. This powerful formation goes with the Great Compassion Mantra:

ན་མོ་རཏྣ་ཏྲ་ཡཱ་ཡ།

ན་མཿ ཨཱརྻ་ཛྙཱ་ན་སཱ་གཱ་ར།

བཻ་རོ་ཙ་ན་བྱཱུ་ཧ་ར་ཛཱ་ཡ།

ཏ་ཐཱ་ག་ཏཱ་ཡ།

ཨརྷ་ཏེ་སམྱཀྶཾ་བུདྡྷཱ་ཡ། ན་མཿ

སརྦ་ཏ་ཐཱ་ག་ཏེ་བྷྱཿ ཨརྷད་བྷྱཿ

སམྱཀྶཾ་བུདྡྷེ་བྷྱཿ ན་མཿ

ཨཱརྻ་ཨ་ཝ་ལོ་ཀི་ཏེ་ཤྭ་རཱ་ཡ།

བོ་དྷི་སཏྭཱ་ཡ། མཧཱ་སཏྭཱ་ཡ།

མཧཱ་ཀཱ་རུ་ཎི་ཀཱ་ཡ། ཏདྱ་ཐཱ།

ཨོཾ་དྷ་ར་དྷ་ར། དྷི་རི་དྷི་རི།

དྷུ་རུ་དྷུ་རུ། ཨི་ཊྚེ། ཝི་ཊྚེ།

ཙ་ལེ་ཙ་ལེ། པྲ་ཙ་ལེ་པྲ་ཙ་ལེ།

གུ་སུ་མེ། གུ་སུ་མེ།
ཝཱ་རེ་ཨི་ལི་མི་ལི།
ཙི་ཏི་ཛྭ་ལ་མཱ་པ་ན་ཡེ་སྭཱཧཱ།

NAMO RATNA TRA YA YA/ NAMA ARYA JANA SAGARA/ VAIROCHANA VYUHA RAJAYA/ TATHAGATAYA/ ARHATE SAMYAK SAM BUDDHAYA/ NAMA SARVA TATHAGATE BAYE ARHATE BAYE/ SAMYAK SAM BUDDHE BAYE/ NAMO ARYA AVALOKITE SHORAYA/ BODHI SATTVAYA/ MAHA SATTVAYA MAHA KARUNI KAYA/ TEYATHA/ OM DHARA DHARA/ DHIRI DHIRI/ DHURU DHURU/ ITTE VATTE/ CHALE CHALE/ TRACHALE TRACHALE/ KUSUME KUSUME VARE/ ILI MILI/ CHITI DZOLA MAPANAYE SVAHA

Please see the guidebook Appendix for links to audio recordings of the Compassion Mantra and Great Compassion Mantra.

The seed syllable of Avalokiteshvara is SHIR ཧྲཱིཿ . The seed syllable contains the full energy of the whole mantra. You can visualise the seed syllable ཧྲཱིཿ on a translucent moon cushion and a 1000-petal white lotus in meditation. The seed syllable ཧྲཱིཿ emanates the light of wisdom in five colours: blue, orange-yellow, white, green, and red.

Amitabha — Buddha of Infinite Light

Avalokiteshvara's crown is always adorned with his teacher, Amitabha, Buddha of Infinite Light. As one of the five Celestial Buddhas (or *Tathagatas*), Amitabha's colour is red, representing the purified element of fire, the red light of discriminating awareness that transcends the aggregate (*skandha*) of perception (thoughts). 'Discriminating' here means seeing the sharp details of all phenomena the way they are without being judgemental. Buddha Amitabha's symbol is also a lotus, again representing purity.

Akshobhya — Celestial Buddha

On the east (front) petal is the Celestial Buddha Akshobhya, whose colour is blue, representing the transcendental element of water and the purified aggregate of form (body). Buddha Akshobhya's symbol is the *vajra* or the thunderbolt, representing immovability or indestructibility. Such immovability is founded on the direct perception of reality that can thus withstand the critical attitude of the intellectual mind, which focuses on what is wrong with every phenomenon.

Ratnasambhava — Celestial Buddha

On the south petal is the Celestial Buddha Ratnasambhava, whose colour is yellow, representing the transcendental element of earth and the yellow wisdom light of equanimity that transcends the aggregate of feelings. Buddha Ratnasambhava's symbol is the wish-fulfilling jewel, representing dignity and the absence of poverty.

Vairocana — Celestial Buddha

On the west petal is the Celestial Buddha Vairocana, whose colour is white, representing the purified element of space and the wisdom of all-pervading vision, free from any centralised perspective. Such a complete sense of openness brings the purified aggregate of consciousness. Buddha Vairocana's symbol is the eight-spoked wheel which represents a state that transcends the limitations of direction and time.

Amoghasiddhi — Celestial Buddha

On the north petal is the Celestial Buddha Amoghasiddhi, whose colour is green, representing the purified element of wind and the wisdom of transcending the aggregate of mental formations (concepts). Buddha Amoghasiddhi is symbolised in the Compassion Mandala by the sword, representing the sharp intelligence that swiftly cuts down the illusions of the mind so as to see what's actually happening. Such is the way to efficiently remove obstacles so that the fulfilment of actions is firmly secured.

The presence of the five Celestial Buddhas in the Compassion Mandala demonstrates that the Buddha of Compassion, Avalokiteshvara, has the fully enlightened qualities of all Buddhas.

Indestructible Protection

The eight-petal lotus, representing the depth of the centre of the heart chakra, is cocooned by a seamless wall of the golden light of *vajra*, which is indestructible. The indestructible protection of the mind comes from the thorough realisation of wisdom. Such wisdom is based on direct perception of the nature of all creation and dissolution — which, in turn, is supported by a solid foundation of the thorough, intellectual investigation of truth.

Sense Offerings

Skirting the palace is a red ledge with goddesses holding pure offerings of drinking water, bathing water, perfume, flowers, incense, lamps of lights, food, and sound instruments, as well as mirrors (representing eye-sense offering), cymbals (representing ear-sense offering), perfume (representing nose-sense offering), fruits (representing tongue-sense offering), and silk scarves (representing body-sense offering). These offerings are pure because they are enjoyed as the spontaneous result of multiple causes and conditions of the moment, as opposed to being objects with inherent qualities.

Garudas and Dharma Wheels

On top of the four palace doors are the four *Garudas*, from whose mouths drip strings of jewels, representing the pure speech of wisdom teachings. In front of the four palace doors are the four archways, adorned with 11 layers of segments, each resting on four pillars. On top of the four archways, each flanked by a pair of deers, are four *Dharma wheels* that emit clouds of compassion. The clouds of compassion shower down flowers of wisdom nectar, suitable for individual sentient beings' mental dispositions.

Merit Symbols

The green landscape outside the palace is filled with a rich body of victory banners (symbolising spiritual attainment), parasols (symbolising spiritual powers), and trees full of treasures. They symbolise the ocean-like merits accumulated by Buddhas and Bodhisattvas, who work diligently day and night to perform virtuous deeds in order to share the resulting material and spiritual wealth with all sentient beings.

The Pure Realm

The celestial palace and landscape sit on top of a 1000-petal lotus, again symbolising the pure realm. The pure realm is protected by a seamless cocoon of the indestructible, golden light of *vajra*, which, in turn, is surrounded by the five-coloured wisdom fire that transforms mental afflictions into the light of wisdom.

Generate Pure Space with the Compassion Mandala

To generate a pure space for attaining wisdom insights with this deck of cards, the authors recommend you place a Compassion Mandala on the altar or a clean table in front of you. Chant the Compassion and/or Great Compassion Mantra—as an invocation of Avalokiteshvara and all Buddhas and Bodhisattvas of the ten directions—three times. Then, offer the mandala as a pure realm to Buddhas and Bodhisattvas. Chanting these mantras also awakens seeds of compassion in all sentient beings, and the pure realm of the mandala offering is for all sentient beings to share. This is a great way to accumulate merits. You can do this with the following prayers:

Homage

The 1000 arms serving as the 1000 universe-ruling emperors.

The 1000 eyes manifesting as the 1000 Buddhas of our times, who teach and show the way to whatever others desire.

To you, Avalokiteshvara, Buddha of Compassion, I pay homage.

Compassion Mantra

OM MANI PEME HUM

(Repeat 7, 21, 108 times, or as many times as you can.)

Great Compassion Mantra

NAMO RATNA TRA YA YA/ NAMA ARYA JANA SAGARA/ VAIROCHANA VYUHA RAJAYA/ TATHAGATAYA/ ARHATE SAMYAK SAM BUDDHAYA/ NAMA SARVA TATHAGATE BAYE ARHATE BAYE/ SAMYAK SAM BUDDHE BAYE/ NAMO ARYA AVALOKITE SHORAYA/ BODHI SATTVAYA/ MAHA SATTVAYA MAHA KARUNI KAYA/ TEYATHA/ OM DHARA DHARA/ DHIRI DHIRI/ DHURU DHURU/ ITTE VATTE/ CHALE CHALE/ TRACHALE TRACHALE/ KUSUME KUSUME VARE/ ILI MILI/ CHITI DZOLA MAPANAYE SVAHA

(Repeat 3, 7, or 21 times.)

Please see the guidebook Appendix for audio recordings of the Compassion Mantra and Great Compassion Mantra.

Mandala Offering

This ground, anointed with perfume, strewn with flowers,

adorned with Mount Meru, four continents, the sun and the moon.

I imagine this as a Buddha-field and offer it.

May all living beings enjoy this pure land!

Holy and perfect, pure lama, from the clouds of compassion

that form in the skies of your Dharmakaya wisdom,

please release a rain of vast and profound Dharma,

precisely in accordance with the needs of those to be trained.

IDAM GURU RATNA MANDALA KAMA NIRYA TAYAMI

Dedication

Through this virtue,

may I quickly accomplish the state of Avalokiteshvara

and establish all beings, without exception, in that state.

Bestow without obstruction the fulfilment of all wishes,

like a wish-fulfilling gem or an excellent vase.

Think that the whole universe and the beings and objects within it are now completely pure, made entirely of five-coloured wisdom light.

You can offer the mandala as many times as you like in a day. In the Tibetan Buddhist tradition, one of the preliminary practices before an elaborate meditational retreat is offering the mandala 100,000 times within one to three months. This is to accumulate sufficient merits so that the retreat is fruitful in generating wisdom realisations and attaining enlightened aspiration.

A Meditation on Loving Kindness and Compassion

It is good to have a Compassion Mandala on your table or altar, to generate positive energy in the room or space. It is also good to perform the Mandala Offering ritual at the beginning of this meditation session in preparation.

Step 1. Posture

You can do this meditation sitting or standing. If standing, make sure your feet are parallel and about shoulder-width apart. If sitting in a chair, make sure the chair is not too high. It's good if your feet can be placed comfortably on the ground, parallel to each other, with your knees at about 90 degrees. Try not to lean back in the chair; make sure that your body is light and elevated so that there's no pressure on your tailbone. Allow your centre of gravity to be subtly adjustable and always balanced over where you are standing or sitting. This is a 'moving balance' rather than a static one.

Step 2. Pure Motivation

Generate pure motivation by thinking throughout this meditation, "I want to empower myself with loving kindness and compassion, so I can attain full enlightenment and bring all sentient beings also to that state (or so that I can be a wonderful person for others)."

Step 3. Breathing

Open your arms and raise them slowly with your palms facing upwards as if embracing the sunlight of loving kindness. Imagine the central line of your body extending upwards and downwards comfortably. Bring your palms together. Move your hands slowly down in front of your body, with palms facing downwards. Allow all your muscles to settle into a neutral tone, neither slack nor tense. This is achieved by allowing your centre of gravity to be spontaneously adjustable so that you are always balanced where you are sitting or standing.

Repeat this a few times, allowing your breathing to be natural and comfortable.

Step 4. Calming the Coarse-Level Mind

Bring your mind back to peace by thinking, "It is now a quiet time for the earth, water, fire and wind elements in my body. It is now a quiet time for my eye, ear, nose, tongue, body, mental sense power and sense consciousness."

Step 5. Focusing on the Compassion Mantra

Focus your mind on the Compassion Mantra:

OM MANI PEME HUM

ཨོཾ་མ་ཎི་

Chant the mantra either out loud, quietly, or in your mind 7, 21, 108 times, or as many times as you can. You can count with a mala of beads if you have one.

When chanting the mantra, hold in your mind a subtle intention of loving kindness towards all sentient beings. Or you can visualise the seed syllable SHIR ཤྲཱི྅ sitting on a translucent moon disc, which, in turn, sits on a 1000-petal white lotus. Visualise that the seed syllable ཤྲཱི྅ is made of five-coloured wisdom light and is also emanating fine rays of five-coloured light: blue, orange-yellow, white, green, and red.

Step 6. Focusing on Loving Kindness and Compassion

Fill your mind and body with the joyful energy of loving kindness by counting the blessings in life you have taken for granted, however small and common they may appear to be:

- Think of all those who have contributed to your living substances and wellbeing through their daily diligence.
- Think of those who have done something special for you today.
- Think of the good qualities of the people related to present issues in your life.

Think beautiful words of gratitude for them.

Complete your meditation with generous wishes for all sentient beings to attain the true happiness of enlightenment, particularly those you think of often lately.

You can do this meditation with the cards *(40.) Mother Sentient Beings, (41.) Gratitude*, or *(50.) Empowerment* in front of you. You can also read or contemplate the discussion in the section of this guidebook called 'How to Cultivate Enlightened Aspiration?'

At this point, it is good to offer the mandala again with gratitude towards the Buddhas and Bodhisattvas for their teachings and protection.

Step 7. Dedicating Merits

Dedicate the merits of this short meditation to the enlightenment of all sentient beings and to those who come to your mind.

Step 8. Wake up Properly from the Meditation

Wake up by wiggling your fingers and toes and leave the past behind. Drink some water. Feel completely renewed and ready to take a fresh look at things so as to make a humble contribution to the wellbeing of others.

It's good to take short 5 to 10-minute meditations (steps 1–8) every day to keep your mind fresh and your body filled with positive energy. It's important to make it easy and enjoyable.

Generating Wisdom Insights with the Cards

After a meditation on loving kindness and compassion, you are in a good position to work with the cards in the deck to help you address a situation or challenge you may be experiencing.

Hold the situation in your mind, generate pure motivation, draw cards in any way you feel comfortable, or go through them and pick out a few you think are relevant. Read the messages and then review your attitude towards the situation.

Finish the session by dedicating the merits of your virtuous thoughts to the enlightenment of all sentient beings. Keep this short. You can always come back to this process again.

Please note: The Compassion Mandala is a sacred image. Please do not place the cards with this image casually on a chair or on the ground where people might sit on them or walk over them. Always place them in a high, dry place with respect. If you prefer to work with your cards while sitting on the floor, make sure the cards are placed on a scarf or tablecloth.

Have fun and enjoy!

Ritual to Purify Negative Karma

The Power of the Foundation

Place the Compassion Mandala in front of you on a clean table or altar. Offer the mandala to all Buddhas and Bodhisattvas, and perform steps 1–8 of the Meditation on Loving Kindness and Compassion. If you feel comfortable, have the cards *(1.) Innocent Mind, (4.) Karma, (22.) Remorse, (35.) Guilt,* and *(45.) Dissolution* in front of you. They carry the wisdom message that all negative karma can be purified. This setting provides refuge and strength for purifying negative karma.

The Power of Eradication or Confession

Imagine you have the Buddha of Compassion and all the Buddhas and enlightened beings in front of you. Generate a strong wish for all sentient beings to attain the happiness of enlightenment, and set this as your motivation for this practice. Contemplate the negative effects of non-virtuous actions and generate a strong intention to purify them so as to be free from these negative effects.

The Power of Turning Away from Faults

Generate a strong intention not to repeat non-virtuous actions.

The Power of Applying Remedies

This practice involves accumulating merits as remedies. The following practices are powerful ways to generate merits:

- Pay homage and make offerings to the Buddha of Compassion.
- Offer the mandala to Buddhas and all enlightened beings, and share the pure realm with all sentient beings.
- Request help from the Buddha of Compassion to purify negative karma.

Chant the Compassion Mantra *"OM MANI PEME HUM"* as many times as you can, and/or chant the Great Compassion Mantra 21 times, holding a subtle intention of loving kindness towards all sentient beings and wishing all sentient beings be free from negative karma.

Contemplate the innocent nature of mind and thus the impermanent nature of negative karma.

Generate the aspiration to attain enlightenment.

Dedicate the merits of this practice to the enlightenment of all sentient beings and to the purification of negative karma.

The negative karma to purify with the four powers are all mental, verbal, and physical actions performed since the beginningless time until now. These can be actions we have done ourselves, caused others to do, or rejoiced in others' doing, especially those performed with respect to spiritual gurus, teachers, and parents. You can then also focus on a particular non-virtuous habit that you want to renounce or a particular action that you want to purify.

Chanting the Great Compassion Mantra is a very powerful way to purify any negative karma. If you chant the Great Compassion Mantra 21 times every day and practise this four-power meditation, you can definitely trust that all your negative karma accumulated since the beginningless time will be completely purified.

Keep the session short and focused. You can choose to do some or even just one of the options for accumulating the merits listed above in each session.

PART III
CARD MESSAGES

1. INNOCENT MIND

Actions leave imprints in your mind that dissolve like writing on water. Thus, you have the ability to change your habits.

Everyone's natural state of mind is pure and innocent. Marks of past experience start to dissolve as soon as they are generated. Even deeper carvings—from repeated actions that have become a habit—disappear without a trace as long as the repetition has been stopped for long enough. For those suffering the effects of non-virtuous deeds, the way to attain happiness is to replace our non-virtuous with virtuous actions. As the mental imprints of non-virtuous deeds dissolve and those of the virtuous ones deepen, one's happiness also swells, like water in a lake during a rainy season.

2. LOVE

Second by second, keep your beautiful mind engaged in the virtue of generating abundance for all sentient beings. This is loving kindness.

At the coarse level, resources are limited. What we can produce verbally and physically takes time to materialise. However, at the level of the subtle mind, whatever is intended is instantaneously generated, moment by moment. Thus, the capacity of the mind is infinite because love is infinite. Motivated by the intention of loving kindness, the pure realm—which offers great riches for all sentient beings—is instantaneously visualised. This is the Compassion Mandala. Such a beautiful universe, full of material and spiritual riches, is created and sustained by Compassion Mantras. So, let's engage our beautiful minds in the virtue of creating a rich and loving universe for all sentient beings.

3. MANIFESTATION

Creation begins with ideas. Choose which ideas to contemplate, so you can generate a fulfilling life.

Whatever we repeatedly portray in our minds manifests as the words we say to people. What we constantly say becomes what we manifest physically. Whatever our subtle mind has never come across is not produced. What we have stopped engaging our minds with dissipates over time. Therefore, the manifestation of happiness starts with searching for and establishing the meaning of happiness to portray. The secret of building happiness is to know which thoughts and images to familiarise yourself with and which ones to abandon. Therefore, the sooner you start to search for your answer, the better.

4. KARMA

Just because your past wrong deeds have led to an unfavourable situation doesn't mean you have to let yourself suffer. Respond positively and make virtuous choices in each present moment.

Karma is not fate. Everyone deserves happiness—both temporary and ultimate happiness—despite what we have done in the past. Actions leave imprints in your mind that dissolve like writing on water; thus, everyone has the potential to change. So don't let your friends suffer just because they did something non-virtuous due to ignorance. Similarly, don't settle down to live with suffering yourself. Take every second as an opportunity to be born completely anew and virtuous. Leave the suffering behind with the past that no longer exists, and take the opportunity to rise up to virtue in every new moment.

5. PRAYERS

Tangible happiness is accumulated second by second at the subtle-mind level. Every moment, direct your attention towards wishing that others attain true happiness.

Tangible changes in the mind and body are accrued second by second at the subtle mental level. Every single second in which our mind is peacefully concentrating on virtuous images and wishes will manifest as happiness and blessings in our tangible life, sooner or later. All tangible sufferings reflect the lost seconds in which a lack or loss of concentration on virtue at the subtle mental level occurred. This is when the mind falls into the trap of visualising problems and suffering. So, make all your seconds count. Second by second, direct your attention towards the blessings in life. How many seconds in a day is your mind abiding in the tranquillity of compassionate prayers for all sentient beings?

6. VIRTUE

Virtue is built on a stable attitude of non-harm towards others. It takes training to develop such an attitude. This is the best investment of your time because all happiness comes from virtue.

Loving kindness is wishing others happiness. Compassion is wishing others freedom from suffering. Great loving kindness is wishing for all sentient beings to attain the ultimate happiness of full enlightenment or 'omniscient mind'. Great compassion is wishing all sentient beings to be free from the suffering of birth, ageing, sickness, and death, which include all types of suffering. These are virtuous mental factors. When motivated by these virtuous mental factors, our mental, verbal, and physical actions are virtuous. Virtuous actions are positive karma that generates happiness. A virtuous mental state is one that single-pointedly holds a subtle intention of loving kindness and compassion towards all sentient beings. The way to build happiness is by training the mind to abide in the bliss of a virtuous mental state.

7. DEDICATION

Dedication preserves the fruits of your hard work.
So, make sure you dedicate all your merits to the best cause
— the enlightenment of all sentient beings.

For a virtuous deed to generate great merits, it needs to be completed with dedication. Dedication is like harvesting the fruits of hard work and storing them well so they're not lost in the field. The best dedication of the merits of virtuous actions is to the enlightenment of all sentient beings. This way, the positive effects of each virtuous deed ripple continuously until all sentient beings attain full enlightenment. So, make dedication your favourite habit. After each good action, however insignificant it might seem, immediately dedicate the merits to the enlightenment of all sentient beings. Also, at the end of each day, make it a habit to dedicate the merits of all your virtuous actions performed since the beginningless time to the enlightenment of all sentient beings. Dedication itself is a virtuous action. So, enjoy!

8. SPECIFICS

Your current situation may appear to be just like that typical case. However, it can never be. Pay attention to the specifics and crucial details of what is happening now.

Conceptual thinking is based on generic images or abstract meanings. Reality is a situation with specific details. Direct perception can be illustrated as seeing a specific situation as it is instead of trying to fit the specific situation into a generic category. The former leads to relevant actions at the right time. The latter is misleading when responding to a specific situation because the ready-made plan for a general category of situations does not take into account all the crucial details.

9. IMPRESSION

When you think of someone, the image in your mind is your impression of that person based on past encounters. It is not the actual person.

Your mental image of a person is your impression of that person based on snapshots of past encounters. The conceptual mind comprehends a person via this mental image. The actual person, however, is not a static image. The actual person evolves dynamically with each new experience, second by second. So, when you think of someone, remind yourself that you are thinking only of an impression of that person, based on incomplete information. Then, the appearance of a negative impression in the mind will not lead to negative comments about that person, which imply that person is inherently that way. The way to accumulate positive karma is to wish for the person to grow free from the faults you perceive in your negative impression of them. Every time we have a negative thought about someone, it's a good opportunity to contemplate how someone (ourselves, for example) can be free from such faults.

10. FAULTS

When you see faults in others, this is a golden opportunity to investigate whether the judgement standards you hold in your mind are valid.

The fault I see in my venerable guru is a reflection of the imperfection of my own mind. The fault is, by nature, a mental impression of my guru in that specific situation, generated by my own mind. The mind that habitually thinks of kindness sees kindness in others. The mind that habitually judges sees faults in others. Knowing that my guru doesn't actually have that fault, I look for bumps in my own mind to be smoothed out. As a result, I set myself free from the arbitrary standard I have set up for judgement. A faultless world is one filled with appreciation, gratitude, and loving images of all sentient beings.

11. OBSERVATION

The first person who is emotionally disturbed by a negative comment is the one who makes the comment. You can only observe factual information when your mind remains calm and unbiased from judgement.

Making judgemental comments about someone is rude. It's like labelling the person with a fixed opinion based on snapshot impressions taken at specific occasions. However, giving up being judgemental does not mean giving up observation of factual information. As a matter of fact, being judgemental obstructs the unbiased view of what's occurring. Factual information can only be observed with a mind that is free from judgemental comments on people and objects. This is because the first person who is emotionally disturbed by a negative comment is the one who makes the comment. Thus, decisions based on observations that are free from mental comments about people and objects are actually made with much better clarity in mind — they are less biased.

12. THE SELF

Labelling yourself with inherent qualities based on past occurrences only limits you to the past, which is no longer relevant. Choose a fresh perspective and virtuous attitude in each new moment.

How do you perceive yourself? As a stockpile of various inherent qualities? Or as a mental and physical continuum, rising moment by moment due to specific causes and conditions? The image of yourself in your mind is constructed with jigsaw pieces of impressions from past events, as well as the wish to modify or improve those impressions. If you hold yourself as inherently this way or that way based on such an image, then you are limited by specific past events that are no longer relevant. If you see that you have a chance to be born anew every single moment, then you are free to adopt a virtuous attitude freshly every single moment. This is the way to build a happy life.

13. HAPPINESS

Pleasant mental and physical feelings are temporary and conditional happiness. Attain true happiness by training your mind to abide in the tranquillity of virtue.

Mental and physical pleasant feelings are, by nature, the temporary relief of mental and physical unpleasant feelings. For example, eating brings happy feelings because it relieves the discomfort of being hungry. It's conditional happiness because if one is already full, eating more food will generate discomfort in the body. The relief is temporary because, after a few hours, the hungry feeling comes back, demanding even more attention. True happiness is attained by training the mind to abide in the tranquillity of virtue. A virtuous mental state is a sustained, subtle intention of kindness towards all sentient beings. Practise taking a 15-minute break every day from chasing temporary relief, and enjoy this tranquillity of the virtuous mind. It is really blissful!

14. PAST

*Dwelling in memories means living in illusion.
Embrace the opportunity of the present moment to
generate a happy life for everyone.*

Are you constantly reliving an upsetting situation that occurred yesterday? The reality is that the incident no longer exists, just like all past events. Even if you go back to the same location with the same people, you won't be able to reconstruct what occurred in exactly the same way. Because both the environment and the people have evolved since yesterday. Yesterday's occurrence was due to a specific set of causes and conditions that are not replicable. What you are replaying over and again is your impression of the occurrence yesterday — like watching a video recording taken from a particular angle. Furthermore, as you are replaying the recording, you are editing it with colours of negative feelings such as self-pity, sadness, and anger. So, what do you choose to do with your precious human life? Hide in a corner editing an old video recording, getting comfortable with negative feelings so that you become more prone to them? Or step out to the wisdom sunlight of self-empowerment to build a rich and beautiful world for all your friends and family?

15. PLANNING

A plan is a mental simulation of how to respond to what's likely to happen. There's no need to be rigidly attached to your plans. Respond spontaneously to the real-life situation that is happening now.

A plan is not future reality, because it is made before the time when all the information regarding the future situation is available. So, there's no need to be upset because things are not evolving according to your plan. A plan is useful as a mental simulation of your preferred course of response to what's likely to happen in future, given the information available now. Planning can also involve researching and acquiring relevant knowledge about your situation. However, dwelling too much on making your plan work leads to narrow-minded rejection of the reality of a broad range of possibilities. Knowing that planning is about learning, the courageous ones surf the waves of uncertainty with spontaneous decisions in response to the living situation now.

16. THE PRESENT MOMENT

The present moment is the only one that is worth your attention.
The last moment is over, and the next is not yet born.

The wise ones focus their attention on this one single moment. This is when and where it all happens. This opportunity presented in the present moment does not stay; the moment constantly evolves forward. Those who learn to stay or move forward with this present moment capture everything life has to offer. The mind that dwells in past events or future plans is not in touch with what's going on now and thus misses the only opportunity to create happiness for oneself and others. To catch this opportunity, one trains the mind to abide in the virtuous intention of loving kindness towards all, be they friends or enemies.

Despite what the external conditions are and how you feel internally, single-pointedly focus on generating virtue — mentally, verbally, and physically. This way, you will not have any problems from the past, nor any worries about the future, because you have taken all the opportunities to generate a bright present moment. This present moment is the only moment there ever is — because the past is the last present moment that's over, and the future is the next present moment that's not yet born.

17. DISTURBANCE

*Minor irritation, if not checked, can blow into burning anger.
Always schedule time to ease your mind back to peace.*

Take a moment to examine your mental state. Are you feeling emotionally disturbed? It's important to ease your mind back to a healthy state so that the irritation does not blow into burning anger.

First, bring your mind back to peace by thinking, "It is now a quiet time for the earth, water, fire, and wind elements in my body. It is now a quiet time for my eye, ear, nose, tongue, body, and mental sense power and sense consciousness." Then, fill your mind and body with the joyful energy of loving kindness by counting all the blessings in your life you have taken for granted, however small and common they may appear to be. Think beautiful words of gratitude towards all those who have contributed to your living substances and wellbeing through their daily diligence. Repeat this process until you feel peaceful and confident.

Now you are ready to examine the source of your irritation and see how it is actually your mental impression of the person/situation that is upsetting you, rather than reality, which never stops evolving.

18. MOTIVATION

The most powerful motivation is generated by cultivating great compassion. Cultivate great compassion by always setting the pure intention of benefiting others in what you do.

The most important factor for spiritual wellbeing is the right motivation. People with good spirits are positively motivated. The most powerful motivation is great compassion. Cultivating great compassion forms the path towards full enlightenment. Pure motivation is what separates the virtuous from the non-virtuous. So, observe how you can be of help to others in your daily work. Let wishing that others be happy and free from suffering be the profound motivation for your daily activities. Make a good habit of generating this pure motivation as soon as you wake up every morning. This is the key to living a meaningful life.

19. COMPASSION

Great compassion is based on pure intention that is free from emotional entanglement with those you are trying to help. You can be of most service to others when you are at peace within yourself.

Compassion is not about enduring other people's harm. Compassion means facilitating others to accomplish virtue. If spending time with your friends only gives them opportunities to repeat a bad habit, then the best way to help your friends is to cut yourself clean from the emotional entanglement. Seek peace and empowerment; offer yourself mental space to enjoy the blessings in life. Those who have accomplished happiness literally left suffering behind and engaged themselves in happiness. After you have become peaceful yourself, you will be empowered to offer real help to your friends.

20. HUMBLENESS

Refrain from the need to defend your own sense of righteousness. To support fruitful conversations, cultivate an attitude of humbleness.

Humbleness is the opposite of pride. Pride is a sense of being superior to others. It often manifests as a deep-seated attitude of "I can't be wrong". As a result, fruitful discussions are often jeopardised because our attention is steered away from the actual topic towards defending that we are right. With a humble manner, one always considers oneself to be lower than others. True humbleness shows as an attitude of not feeling the need to defend that "I am right" or "I'm not completely wrong" or to establish that "I know that already".

21. REJOICING

One of the best-kept secrets for attaining happiness is to immediately congratulate your rivals. Rejoice in their success and everyone else's, including your own.

Rejoicing is the antidote to jealousy. Jealousy is a feeling of disturbance in response to seeing or hearing good things happening to others. Rejoicing is feeling happy about good things happening to others. Jealousy leads to mental, verbal, and physical non-virtuous actions that are harmful or offensive towards others. Rejoicing is a virtuous mental factor.

Rejoicing in other people's fortunes and achievements is a wonderful habit to develop. The merits accumulated by rejoicing in other people's virtues are as many as those accumulated by performing the virtues oneself. So let's rejoice in our own happiness and achievements! Let's rejoice in our friends' happiness and achievements! Let's wholeheartedly rejoice in our rivals' happiness and achievements!

The way our minds work is that we project what we want to achieve onto those we admire. Seeing the failed efforts of others only affirms our own insecurity. Therefore, whatever we see happening—or, more accurately, whatever we imagine happening—to others has a huge psychological impact on ourselves. So, if one wants success, one should celebrate everyone's success. Those trying to undermine others are effectively undermining themselves. That's how the law of karma works at a deeper level.

22. REMORSE

Remorse should not become self-punishment or depression. Rather, celebrate that you will no longer repeat the non-virtuous action that caused you to feel remorse.

Remorse is not about devaluing yourself. Neither is it about punishment. It's actually about knowing which behaviours to abandon for the wellbeing of yourself and others.

According to Medicine Buddha's 'Twelve Great Wishes', every single sentient being deserves the best of everything: good health, good wealth, good form, good sense and mental faculties, a peaceful and loving mind, freedom from non-virtuous habits, freedom from all mental and physical pains, the attainment of wisdom realisations, and the attainment of full enlightenment.

So, as soon as you become aware of your wrong deeds, just say sorry, ask for forgiveness, and make a strong mental note not to repeat them. With that, you have put them behind you. It's good to recognise our own wrongdoing. Embarrassment and remorse are virtuous mental factors that discourage us from repeating the non-virtuous. However, sinking down to self-punishing fear is unnecessary. The wise choice is to leave the past as the past and focus your attention on accumulating virtuous merits now.

23. MENTAL AFFLICTIONS

Develop alertness about the mental factors that are present in your mind. When the presence of non-virtuous mental factors is strong, the wise choice is not to say or do anything.

Ignorance, attachment, anger, pride, jealousy, and doubt are the six root mental afflictions. Mental, verbal, and physical activities driven by these mental afflictions are non-virtuous actions. When anger, pride, and jealousy are present in mind, the virtuous mental factors—loving kindness and compassion—are not. They are mutually exclusive. Actions performed with loving kindness and compassion at heart are virtuous. Develop alertness about what mental factors are present in your mind. When the presence of non-virtuous mental factors in the mind is strong, the wise choice is not to say or do anything. Adjust your mental state by first calming down from negative emotions and then meditating strongly on loving kindness and compassion.

24. ATTACHMENT

Extending loving kindness to your partner is the secret to sustaining a healthy relationship.

Attachment is not love. Attachment is founded on the idea that "this benefits me". Love is founded on "this benefits others". Relationships built on attachment fall apart when they cost us too much to maintain. Relationships built on love grow evergreen. Relationships based on attachment are draining. Relationships based on love are life-nourishing. Those who give love generously, without calculating whether or not it is worth it, enjoy an ever-flowing stream of warmth and a joyful home.

25. ANGER

Anger is the culprit behind hurtful behaviour, not the person who is angry. Help yourself and others ease the irritation that leads to being controlled by anger.

If someone is yelling at you, it's because they are overwhelmed by anger. Anger is an afflictive mental state that starts with mounting irritation when something that appears to be very unpleasant and threatening occupies the mind. Anger flares up when the irritation can no longer be contained. When we calm down from anger, we usually experience the realisation that things are not actually that bad. Therefore, there's no need to take it personally when someone is angry at you. Because the object of anger is not you but a mental image in the mind of the other person. Also, there's no need to blame them because they are not inherently that way. Ignorance and anger are the culprits that bring about disharmony. If the two of you work as a team, you can overcome the real enemy by catching the misunderstandings that cause irritation in the first place and clearing them up before you both fall into the afflictive mental state of anger.

26. LETHARGY

Lethargy is a temporary situation. It is not an inherent quality. You can overcome lethargy by engaging in regular nourishment of both your mind and body.

Do you often feel that your body is tired and your mind lacks motivation? This is not an inherent state. It rises at various moments due to specific causes and conditions. However, if you identify with it by thinking "this is how I am", then you are accepting it as a default setting in your mind-computer. In this case, you are letting it leave an increasingly deeper mark in your mind and thus become more prone to the various triggers that draw you into it.

The wise choice is to recognise lethargy's appearance and say no to it firmly. This way, you reset your mind-computer to be free from lethargy. Seek refuge in the powerful virtue of great compassion. Instead of settling down with negative feelings, focus on wishing all sentient beings be protected by the warm heart of loving kindness. Renew the wish every few seconds, accompanied by easy and nurturing activities that support your mental and physical regeneration. Knowing its temporary nature, let lethargy pass without engaging with it. Be determined to break free from it, so you can offer your valuable service to others. Regularly practising mental and physical regeneration is the way to transcend lethargy.

27. SELF-CONSCIOUSNESS

Seeking approval externally is fruitless and energy-draining. Others' disapproval is a projection from your own mind. The right way to gain confidence is to work with a pure intention.

Observe how you apply your energy when you work. How much of your attention is on performing the actual tasks, and how much is applied to leaving a good impression? While being conscientious is a good quality, feeling the need to prove yourself, or worrying about not performing with excellence, is counterproductive. It costs your energy and offers no benefit. It makes your working hours emotionally charged. Not only does it disturb your mental clarity during work, it also slumps you down to a low mood after work.

These negative emotions have their roots in pride and jealousy — mental afflictions to be abandoned if you want to live a fulfilling life. The wise choice is thus to enjoy your work with the pure motivation of benefiting others. Working with a pure intention is the way to ensure that your efforts will bear good fruits for yourself and others. Once we are heading in the right direction, all we need to do is focus on each specific task one at a time and be grateful for the opportunity to learn.

28. ANXIETY

Anxiety is fear due to uncertainty. The way to reduce anxiety about something is to find out more about it. You will be amazed just how much you actually know, and thus can already handle.

Anxiety is the fear of the unknown. If we know exactly what it is—good or bad—we can form an optimal response and be content with it. Therefore, the way to reduce anxiety regarding, for example, an exam or a job interview, is to find out more about it, then formulate and implement action plans based on the known information, step by step. If you practise this, you will be amazed at just how much you already know. This way, strong anxiety is chipped down to faint anxiety, which then dissipates as your confidence grows.

The stronger one is spiritually, the less chance one has of becoming fearful in any situation. Put your hands over your heart and call your own name loudly in your mind three times, with a clear intention that your spiritual energy be focused on virtue and grounded within your body. Focus your mind on the Compassion Mantra "OM MANI PEME HUM" or on grateful thoughts for spiritual nourishment. Take refuge in the virtues of great loving kindness and compassion to grow stronger every day!

29. SOCIAL PRESSURE

Certainty comes from examining situations objectively. Appreciate your external sources of pressure, for they are encouraging you to find mental clarity.

Do you feel pressured to make an uncomfortable choice? The pressure is not external. One feels pressure only if one agrees with at least some of the reasons to make the choice.

Instead of becoming irritated with the external sources of pressure, it is time to sit down and examine the pros and cons of the choice in your own mind. Which uneasy feelings are based on facts? Which are triggered by a totally unrelated issue? Which reason for making the choice is sensible and virtuous? Which is just an unreasonable request?

Certainty comes from peace within one's own mind. Consider the external pressures to be encouragement for you to gain mental clarity by examining the situation objectively.

30. LOSS

One way or another, the money you lost puts food on someone else's table. This someone must be your long-lost family.

Have you just come out of a bad financial deal? The good news is that you have just settled one or more karmic debts. Karmic debts accrue interest; thus, the sooner they are settled, the more peaceful your mind becomes. Be grateful to those who helped bring your money to those you couldn't have reached out to yourself. One way or another, the money you 'lost' puts food on someone else's table and helps to take care of someone else's children. This someone must be your long-lost family. Take a moment to wish that they are enjoying your generous gift.

31. LIMITATION

Any new growth comes from breaking through obstacles. The obstacles are not external. They are reflections of your own limiting beliefs about how things can be done.

Have you been thinking about a dynamic new project that will open your life to new horizons? Does it appear to be financially or otherwise beyond your reach? Do certain aspects of the project make you feel that it will be difficult or troublesome to complete? It's time to formulate the blueprint by investigating it objectively.

First, does this project benefit many others, or how can this project benefit as many beings as possible? Are you determined to do it? Second, if you are determined to do it, how can this project be implemented in stages so that it is feasible financially as you accumulate experience? Third, what skills will be required to handle the difficult aspects of the project? Do you want to acquire these skills or capacities?

Any new growth comes with breaking through obstacles. The obstacles are not external. They are reflections of your own limited mental ideas about how things can be done. If this new direction generates opportunities for those you care about, are you ready to broaden your perspective so that you transcend these limitations? Are you determined to transcend your own limitations so that you can be of better service to mother sentient beings?

32. EXPECTATION

What someone should be able to do is your mental expectation of the person; it may not reflect the reality of what the person could actually do.

Have you been upset because an adult person behaved immaturely? If so, your reason for being angry is unfounded. What someone should be able to do is your mental expectation of the person, not how the person actually is. Your reason for being angry is unfounded because you mistook an immature person as being mature at that point in time. The wise choice is to grant the kind of patience you would to an immature person in this instance. However, be careful not to deduce from this particular incident that the person is always immature; you might be surprised just how very mature they are on the next occasion.

33. TIME TO PUT YOURSELF FIRST?

The compassionate way to help your friends is to share your ideas while respecting their choices. To attain happiness, they must do the right thing of their own will.

Have you become weary of trying to help a friend? Do you feel that being compassionate to them wears you out? The truth is that it takes the support of wisdom to accomplish compassionate deeds. Have you been trying to help your friend or steer them towards the happiness of your own definition? If the latter is true, then it will be wearisome because your efforts will be resisted. Have you been scheduling time to refresh your own mind and body every day? Being compassionate is not the direct cause of tiredness — not knowing when to rest is. Without a proper daily routine to freshly regenerate the mind and body, one would feel tired doing just about anything. To attain happiness, one has to perform virtuous deeds out of one's own will. That's the law of karma. So, the compassionate way to help your friends is to share your ideas while respecting their choices.

34. REGENERATION

The secret ingredient of fulfilment is the capacity to maintain good form. The secret of keeping in good form is nothing more than regular nourishment of both your mind and body.

Have you been skipping meals and reducing your sleep to get more work done? The secret ingredient to fulfilment is actually the capacity to maintain good form, both physically and mentally. The secret of keeping in good form is nothing more than regular nourishment. So, when you are feeling down, simply take a moment to regenerate yourself before jumping to the conclusion that you have this mental issue and that physical problem. It doesn't take long to become regenerated. Do a five-minute meditation on loving kindness and compassion, eat a healthy and nutritious snack and leave the past behind. Feel completely renewed and ready to take a fresh look at things so as to make humble contributions to the wellbeing of others. With better mental clarity, you will be more efficient and thus have ample time to enjoy your meals and sleep.

35. GUILT

Dwelling in guilt only holds you in the past. Focus on generating goodness now. One way to do this is by offering the Compassion Mandala for all sentient beings to enjoy.

Has a particular past wrong action been occupying your mind lately, even though you have processed and cleansed it with various methods? If you have applied the correct methods of the four powers to clear the negative karma of that particular action (see 'Ritual to Purify Negative Karma' in the Introduction), it is very important that you trust the negative karma of the wrong action has been purified. What's happening is that certain events occurring now remind you of the memory of that past action. Therefore, repeated purification of the particular past action does not help; rather, it can become a bait to trap you in the past, which no longer exists. The way to snap out of it is thus to focus your attention on the present.

If you are not sure what particular behaviour is to be corrected now, the wise choice is to respond to both virtuous and non-virtuous environments with virtuous intention. The way to fulfil this is to always check whether your mind is focused on loving kindness and compassion towards all, particularly those who you find irritating. So, instead of feeling bad about yourself whenever the guilt-evoking image occurs, engage your mind in meditation on compassion towards all sentient beings and particularly those you have lately felt uneasy about.

36. ACTIONS

What distinguishes virtuous paths of action from non-virtuous ones are the motivating mental factors. Cultivating virtuous mental factors is thus the key to happiness.

An action that brings positive or negative effects in the future has four aspects: the basis, the attitude that leads to motivation, the implementation of the action, and the culmination of the action. For example, for the negative action of killing, the basis is a sentient being who is alive; the attitude is an afflictive mental factor such as anger or strong attachment, which leads to the motivation to kill; the implementation is the action of killing, either by doing it oneself or asking someone else to do it; the culmination is that the living being is no longer alive due to the action.

The corresponding virtuous action is either to refrain from killing as described above or to save a life. The virtuous action of saving a life is motivated by compassion — wishing that the sentient being be free from the suffering of sickness and death. Cultivating great compassion and abandoning afflictive mental factors is, therefore, the key to accumulating causes for happiness.

37. KARMIC EFFECTS

Negative karma shows up as obstacles that block the source of happiness — the virtuous choice. The way to overcome obstacles is to rely on powerful sources of virtue.

The effects of virtuous actions mature as favourable conditions to perform more virtue; those of non-virtuous actions mature as obstacles to enjoying the blessings of life, as well as triggers for afflictive mental factors to arise. These effects can take the form of external conditions, internal feelings, or inclined responses to the situation at hand. All these are invitations to perform either virtuous or non-virtuous deeds. Despite the external and internal conditions, one still has the choice to perform either. One's own choices in response to external and internal conditions are the main causes of the actions that occur moment by moment. Those overwhelmed by obstacles limit themselves to "I have to ..." Those focusing their attention on cultivating virtue end up performing more virtue.

May all sentient beings take refuge in the Three Jewels of Buddha, Dharma, and Sangha and thus enjoy the courage to choose virtues.

38. EQUANIMITY

The differences between individual sentient beings are superficial.
At the most profound level, all sentient beings have the same nature.
Focus on our similarities to build true happiness.

A sentient being is a living being with consciousness and feelings. All sentient beings include sentient beings in the six realms: the god, demi-god, human, animal, hungry ghost and hell realms. All sentient beings have a natural state of mind that is always pure and innocent; all sentient beings bear the seed of compassion; all sentient beings want happiness; no sentient beings like suffering, and all sentient beings are suffering from ageing, sickness, and death.

So, the differences between individual sentient beings are superficial. At the most profound level, all sentient beings have the same nature. Focusing on the differences limits one's life to narrow-minded selfishness — one ends up with fewer and fewer friends and helping hands. Focusing on the similarities is the foundation to cultivate the wisdom of great compassion — one attains the true happiness of omniscience.

May all those who want happiness build it together so that happiness is irreversibly established for all sentient beings.

39. THREE JEWELS

To access a powerful source of virtue, seek answers in wisdom teachings taught by authentic teachers, and apply them to solving daily life challenges, following the example of advanced practitioners.

Buddha, Dharma, and Sangha are the Three Jewels. Dharma includes 84,000 methods for attaining the wisdom of happiness for sentient beings of various mental and physical dispositions. Buddha is the authentic teacher of Dharma. Sangha includes high-level practitioners of Dharma who set tangible examples of how to attain the true happiness of enlightenment. For those who want happiness and don't want suffering, the Three Jewels are powerful forces of protection and guidance. So, seek protection in the Three Jewels by seeking answers to your daily life challenges in Dharma teachings. The way to accumulate success is by first listening to Dharma teachings, then contemplating their meaning, followed by applying your learning to daily life situations.

40. MOTHER SENTIENT BEINGS

Meditate on everything and everyone who has contributed to sustaining and benefiting you. They are the ones who have provided all your necessities and luxuries through their diligent work every day.

'Mother' is the symbol of the protector of children through loving kindness and compassion. A mother always thinks that her children are the most adorable. She could never stand her children being harmed and would readily risk her own life to protect her children. Take a moment to contemplate all those who have protected us from starvation through their diligent work every day. For example, the rice I eat — who delivered it to my house? Who moved it from the miller to the supermarket? Who milled the rice? Who prepared the soil, grew, and harvested the rice? It's someone I think I don't know and have nothing to do with. What has sustained my life is their honest work and humble wish that someone enjoy what they produce. Even the money I have for purchasing the rice comes from someone who kindly accepted the humble service that I offer.

If we meditate on every single thing that has sustained or benefited us, we can see that all sentient beings have been our mother protectors. So, let's take a moment to imagine the most beautiful Mother's Day card — send love to them all and wish them all the attainment of the true happiness of enlightenment.

41. GRATITUDE

May gratitude towards spiritual gurus and mother sentient beings always be present in my mind, so I can repay their loving protection with the bountiful fruits of my virtues.

Any virtuous deeds I have managed to accomplish are purely due to the kindness of my spiritual gurus and mother sentient beings. Mother sentient beings kindly share their merits with me so that I am provided with good living conditions. My determination to free mother sentient beings from being preyed on by mental afflictions has propelled me forward with every step of accumulating virtues. My gurus kindly protected me from falling into the stupor of being mentally scattered. They shared their ocean amount of merits with me so that my mind could focus on cultivating wisdom. May gratitude towards spiritual gurus and mother sentient beings always be present in my mind so that I can repay their loving protection with the bountiful fruits of virtues.

42. APPRECIATION

The self-grasping mentality eats away at our merits and jeopardises our efforts to attain happiness for ourselves and our friends. Consider whether your motivation is pure or driven by a need to be appreciated.

Did your friend complain that you were not helping them, while all the hard efforts you have made to help them on various occasions flooded back into your mind? Did you get upset at that moment and later feel the sadness of not being appreciated?

Now, before playing with the idea of distancing yourself from your friend, take a moment to examine why you were upset. Did you help your friend because they needed help? Or did you help your friend because you want to be appreciated? Or was it a mixture of the two?

If you didn't need to be appreciated at all, would you still feel upset like you did? Helping someone because they need help comes from compassion, which is virtuous. Helping someone because you feel like being appreciated, however, comes from egocentric mentality, which is non-virtuous. Therefore, what made you upset is not what your friend said but the egocentric or self-grasping mentality. This is how such mental afflictions eat away at our merits and jeopardise our efforts to attain happiness for ourselves and our friends. Therefore, take a moment to thank your friend for exposing the true enemy and for offering you a chance to say no to the self-grasping attitude. If not for our good friends, we would lose all our energies to negative emotions without even being aware of the true culprit.

43. RESPECT

*True loving kindness presents as respect for others,
whatever mental dispositions they may have.
Embrace your friends with your loving tolerance.*

Are you witnessing your friend running headlong into the same trouble they fell into not long ago? Are you feeling upset that your friend could just throw away all the efforts you made together to get them out of a similar situation just recently? The wise response is not to settle down to blaming your friend. Take a look at what they are attached to. Take a look at why they think they're losing it. If they are not ready to give up the attachment, maybe you could help them to see that the deadline they set for themself is actually not that inflexible. Your friend can get back to their senses only when the immediate threat of losing what they hold as dear is gone.

Attachment comes on slower than anger, but it sinks in like oil stains a paper — very hard to remove. True loving kindness presents as respect towards others, whatever mental dispositions they may have. Armed with this loving respect, you can help your friend chip away at the binding rope of attachment so that you can both be free from it.

44. CREATION

External difficulties reflect inner stagnation that stems from an attachment to the past. To create the new, you must first let the old dissolve.

Has it been hard for you to get your new project going? Like you keep bumping into solid walls? Before you put any more effort into creating the new, take a moment to examine the source of the obstruction. The secret ingredient of creation is actually the dissolution of the old. If you are reluctant to cover the old painting, there will be no room for the new image to run the show. Holding on to familiar methods narrows the window for trying out more effective ones. Not letting go of the past is the source of obstacles to generating a new life. The source is not external. External difficulties are only a reflection of inner stagnation. With the source of obstacles intact, effort in new creation only brings disappointment. Instead of losing confidence in your project, take some quiet time to investigate the pros and cons of creating the new. Make sure you take into account the cost of dismantling the old. Or, maybe elements of the past can decorate the new structure, to accommodate those who still need a piece of the old time?

45. DISSOLUTION

Yesterday's creation is gone, just like yesterday's footprints on the beach. New creations are constantly being generated today. Create a bright, new life every day.

Just like the tide of the night wipes out footprints on the beach, so go all creations of yesterday. What lingers is the memory, the mental video that was left on. The sand castle on the beach today is freshly built; although it appears to be the same, it is not the one from yesterday. Those who mistake the mental video as real are impressed with an unchanging castle, and thus live within the confines of yesterday. Only those who consistently get up earlier than the sun, and sustain their observations throughout the day, know the secret — that we are offered a fresh sand canvas to paint a new life every day. So how are you going to paint yourself today? The same as yesterday? Slightly healthier and better looking than yesterday? Or, will you introduce the bold colours of wisdom insights?

46. GENEROSITY

It takes skilful nurturing to grow the sprout of compassion into a magnificent tree. Assess your capacity to give, and take sustainable steps to develop this capacity.

What is a generous giving? It doesn't entirely depend on the amount of giving. If Person A donated one dollar and Person B donated ten dollars, it may seem that Person B's giving is more generous. However, if Person A only has ten dollars, but Person B has a million dollars, then Person A's giving now looks more generous. If Person A has been practising generosity diligently, but Person B has never made a donation before, then Person B's giving is a more daring step towards cultivating virtue.

Therefore, the wisdom about giving is that one should assess one's own capacity to give, and take sustainable steps to develop this capacity. The sprout of compassion is so precious, it takes skilful nurturing for it to grow into a magnificent tree. So let's empower ourselves with training in the virtue of giving by making generous wishes to all sentient beings. Let's wish for all sentient beings to attain the true happiness of enlightenment. With this pure motivation, let's accomplish humble steps of generosity in daily life by giving whatever we can or whatever we are ready to part with.

47. TRUST

It takes trust for your friend to confide in you.
Be compassionate and non-judgemental.

Does your friend need help but they are not open to talk? What keeps a line of communication open is trust. It takes trust for people to confide their problems and feelings in others because people feel hurt when they are judged, especially if wrongly judged publicly. The true non-judgemental attitude comes from the mentality of great compassion, which perceives all sentient beings as of the same nature, and thus treats all sentient beings with equanimity. This attitude leads to the objective discussion of factual occurrences, free from finger-pointing at the actors. This is based on the wisdom that each scene of events has its own particular set of causes and conditions and thus cannot be used as proof of evidence that the actors in the event have these or those inherent qualities.

48. FORGIVENESS

The relationship that lasts a lifetime is due to the magic of forgiveness, not because the partners are faultless.

Separation rarely means the end of a relationship. The one who cares always hangs around. Holding grudges due to pride is childish. It's the obstacle to enjoying opportunities for real growth. Maturity comes when the mind of the conceptual perceiver grows open to the vast space of loving kindness. This protects one from being harmed, because the true nature of one's mind is loving kindness itself. The fact that hurtful feelings fade with time is due to this true nature of the mind. We always heal back to being lovingly kind. Those who stop trusting are the ones who let the old video recording flood the mind and thus constantly relive the nonexistent past. Nothing stands still, be it people or the environment. The reality is that we are starting a new relationship every day. The way to get back to the living situation now is to turn off the old video player and see your partner with a fresh set of eyes — or, more precisely, with a fresh perspective of loving kindness. This is the way to treat yourself and your partner with forgiveness.

49. ENLIGHTENED ASPIRATION

Enlightened aspiration is the determination to attain perfect enlightenment and also to lead all sentient beings to that state. This aspiration is the elixir that transforms a mundane life into an empowering path towards true happiness.

The seed of enlightened aspiration is the compassion in our hearts. We cannot bear for our loved ones to suffer, so we must do something to help relieve their suffering. This seed of compassion sprouts into great compassion once it is moistened by the wisdom of equanimity — seeing the truth that all sentient beings have been our loved ones and protected us in numerous past lives. This sprout of great compassion grows into a giant tree, nourished by the aspiration to repay the kindness of our mother sentient beings and the wisdom that all our loved ones are suffering the endless cycle of birth, ageing, sickness, and death. Out of our burning wish to immediately free our loved ones from this pain, we find determination for self-empowerment, aiming for the capacity to free all sentient beings from all suffering. This capacity is the state of perfect enlightenment.

50. EMPOWERMENT

If full enlightenment appears to be far-fetched, why not bring it closer to home, bit by bit? The best reward for your precious human life is to move closer to—and realise the true happiness of— perfect enlightenment.

What we contemplate, discuss and practise every day becomes closer to our hearts. Every action counts. Therefore, if we are heading in the right direction of true happiness, however slowly we move, we will be closer to it and thus enjoy more and more happiness. The right approach is, therefore, to set our eyes on the ultimate goal of enlightenment and take humble steps to accumulate merits from wherever we are. If we persevere patiently—step by step and second by second—we are guaranteed to reach it. It is a gradual yet clearly taught path with many learnings to enjoy along the way.

51. MENTALITY

The fruits of the egocentric mentality are a mind and body that are prone to suffering. The fruits of the mentality of great compassion are a perfect mind and body that enjoy happiness. Build a fulfilling life through mental transformation.

When our mind is in a virtuous state, the wind energy in our body is positive and nurturing. So, contemplating the enlightened aspiration itself is the most supreme source of good energy. One feels tired when the mind turns away from great compassion and falls back to the self-grasping mentality, with negative images of one's own body. The correct attitude for rejuvenation comes from the enlightened intention of self-empowerment: "I must become healthier physically and mentally so that I can work properly for all sentient beings." The difference is that with the self-empowering attitude, the mind holds a positive image of oneself becoming healthier; with the self-pitying attitude, the mind holds a negative image of one's own body, full of pain and tiredness. When the mind itself is pure and innocent, whatever image we hold about ourselves, we will be shaped into. This is why it is beneficial to visualise the virtuous image of a Buddha and contemplate the enlightened aspiration of a Buddha during meditation. In fact, the secret to keeping the body and mind in perfect condition is, during pleasant moments, to wish that all sentient beings enjoy such happiness and, during painful moments, to wish all sentient beings be free from such suffering.

52. TRANSFORMATION

The self-centred mentality cannot lead to happiness. Attain true happiness by abandoning the self-grasping mentality and assuming the mentality of enlightened aspiration.

With the self-centred mentality, one cannot fulfil the goal of bringing oneself happiness. The mundane objectives of happiness are to accumulate more material wealth and to gain higher social status so that we can enjoy more pleasant things in life and thus be admired by others. Any actions driven by these mundane motivations are bound to attract more and more enemies through jealousy and conflicts of interest and push away all virtuous friends. With fewer and fewer opportunities to perform virtuous actions, one's merits will quickly run out, and thus one will fall into misery due to lack of merits. Conversely, with the enlightened aspiration, one is devoted to working for others' wellbeing. Actions driven by such pure motivation are bound to generate more and more virtuous friends and drive away non-virtuous ones. With more opportunities to perform virtuous actions, one accumulates bountiful causes for future happiness. This is why—in response to the plea of sentient beings concerned about the happiness of oneself and others—Buddha taught the path to attain full enlightenment for the benefit of all sentient beings.

GLOSSARY OF TERMS

Aggregates

The five aggregates are form, feelings, thoughts, compositional factors, and consciousness. The first aggregate, **form**, is the physical aspect of a being. **Feelings, thoughts, and consciousness** are mental aspects of a being. Most of the **compositional factors** also belong to the mental aspect. Based on one or more of these aggregates, a sentient being imputes an 'I' or 'self'.

For example, some sentient beings impute an idea of 'I' based on the physical body. Some impute an 'I' based on mental consciousness. Some impute an 'I' based on all five aggregates. According to the 'Buddhist Wisdom of the Middle Way' tenet, as clarified by Master Nagarjuna, the five aggregates are empty of any inherent nature, rising into existence moment by moment due to specific causes and conditions. Thus, a sentient being—as an imputation based on the aggregates—is free from any inherent qualities and rather rises into existence moment by moment due to specific causes and conditions (karma and effects). Consequently, a sentient being is capable of purifying their aggregates through their choice of action in the present moment and evolving into having the pure aggregates of a Buddha.

The beginningless time

'The beginningless time' refers to the omnipresent nature of the mind. Thoughts and feelings are activities of the mind, not the mind itself. The mind itself is simultaneously cognition and brightness (energy). Thoughts and feelings etc., are momentary events formed in the mind due to causes and conditions.

The concept of time is established when multiple events occur in sequence. An event that has occurred is said to have 'happened in the past'; an event that is currently occurring is 'happening in the present'; an event that is yet to occur when certain causes and conditions mature is referred to as 'will happen in the future'.

The mind is beginningless or omnipresent, because whenever or wherever there is cognition or awareness, there is the mind.

Buddha

Buddha is the state of being reached by a sentient being upon complete purification of two defilements: mental afflictions and the obscuration of view. The first defilement includes mental afflictions such as ignorance, attachment, anger, pride, jealousy, and doubt. With the purification of the first defilement, the sentient being's actions are no longer controlled by such afflictions and thus no longer accumulate the karma leading to the cycle of birth, ageing, sickness, and death. The second defilement is the obscuration of the true nature of existence. With the purification of the second defilement, the sentient being is free from even subtle tendencies for these afflictions to arise at all in their mind.

Causally concordant effects

The causally concordant effects of karma are those that influence what kind of living conditions one will be born into — for example, their life span, health conditions, wealth, faculties, etc. Virtuous actions lead to good health, a longer life span, no immature death (death before life span is reached), good wealth, sharp mental and sense faculties, etc. Non-virtuous actions lead to the opposite.

Coarse-level existence

This refers to the state of mind when a sentient being is engaged in elaborate mental, verbal, and physical activities. At this level, the movement of wind energy is like an ocean with big waves.

Conceptual mind

The conceptual mind is established when we name an object because it performs a useful function relative to the mind perceiving it, which is now established as 'I'. Our innate ignorance sees this perceiver as being independent of the object of observation. Such an inherently existing perceiver, 'I', then gives every object a name and specifies how these objects are related to each other and how useful they are to 'I'. A web of elaboration derives thereafter, habitually forming judgement about everything and everyone from that centralised perception of 'I'. Such is mental activity at the conceptual level, based on ignorance. Our root ignorance is holding this 'I' as being an independent entity. This then prompts us to develop an attitude of self-importance and self-cherishing.

The reality is that the existence of the perceiver, 'I', depends on the object of observation. The perceiver and the perceived appear and disappear interdependently and simultaneously. Thus, for each object of observation, a different perceiver arises — dependent upon the object of observation. The nature of 'I' assumed by such a perceiver thus rises moment by moment, depending on causes and conditions.

Environmental effects

The environmental effects of karma are those effects that influence what kind of worldly environment one will be born into — for example, the richness of the soil, the condition of the landscape, the potency of food and medicine, the weather, the cleanliness of the environment, etc. Virtuous actions lead to rebirth into pleasant and rich living environments. Non-virtuous actions lead to rebirth into unpleasant and poor living environments.

Equanimity

The cognitional aspect of the primordial mind works like a mirror, showing what is in front of it precisely and clearly the way it is — this is described as 'mirror-like wisdom'. At this profound level, the mind sees all phenomena as being of the same nature, as they are — a formation of the mind. This is the wisdom of equanimity. This perception is pervasive or omnipresent, like an open space with no centre and no edge.

Things become unequal only at the conceptual level, with an innate ignorant view. Such a view is conducted in relation to a centralised perspective of 'I'. At this level, 'equanimity' refers to the idea that all sentient beings are equal in at least the following senses:

- All sentient beings have the same natural state of mind that cannot be permanently stained.

- All sentient beings have the seed of compassion.

- All sentient beings enjoy happiness, in terms of the mental and physical sense of ease.

- All sentient beings avoid suffering, in terms of the mental and physical sense of pain.

- All sentient beings experience the effects of their virtuous and non-virtuous actions.

In the context of meditational concentration, equanimity refers to the mind being in balance, free from mental excitement and dullness.

Fruition effects

The fruition effects of karma are the effects that influence what kind of body a sentient being will be born into in a future life. There are six realms or six types of bodies one can be born into: god, demi-god, human, animal, hungry ghost, and hell being. Virtuous actions lead to rebirth in the upper realms of gods, demi-gods, and humans. Non-virtuous actions lead to rebirth in the lower realms of animals, hungry ghosts, and hell beings.

Karma

Karma is an action. All actions bring future experiences or 'karmic effects' for the actor — this is the law of karma. A complete path of action has four aspects: basis, attitude, action, and culmination.

For example, the path of the physical action of saving life has the following four elements:

- **Basis:** The basis of saving life is a being who is alive and in danger.

- **Attitude:** Perceiving correctly that the living being is a living being whose life is in danger, motivated by compassion or great compassion, one generates a desire to save the life of the living being.

- **Action:** The performance of saving life is either to do it oneself or to cause someone else to do it.

- **Culmination:** The living being's life is no longer in danger.

The path of action of a kind thought has the following four elements:

- **Basis:** The basis of a kind thought is a living being towards whom one can extend a kind thought.
- **Attitude:** With correct perception, motivated by compassion or great compassion, one generates the desire to, for example, encourage or comfort the living being, thinking such thoughts as "how nice it would be if they were more confident or cheerful."
- **Action:** The performance is having the thought.
- **Culmination:** The culmination is a determination or decision to do something to encourage or comfort the living being.

Mahayana teachings

The path of Buddhist practice for sentient beings aspiring to attain full enlightenment for the benefit of all sentient beings is called the Mahayana path. Mahayana teachings are about the Mahayana path.

Mental disposition

The mental disposition of a sentient being refers to their beliefs and mental habits formed through past learning, experience, and choice of actions. One's mental disposition affects one's choice of actions when confronted by virtuous and non-virtuous influences. Buddha's teachings contain as many as 84,000 different practices to lead sentient beings with different mental dispositions to the same ultimate state of full enlightenment.

Mental factors

For the mind to form an action, there need to be a number of mental elements working simultaneously. There needs to be a 'primary mind' which apprehends the mere entity of the object of engagement. Accompanying the primary mind, there need to be various mental factors that are defined as 'the aspect of awareness that engages with its object with different functions of awareness.' For example, the moment a mother decides to feed her baby, there is a primary mind that grasps the matter of whether the baby needs feeding. Accompanying this primary mind, there are at least six mental factors:

- **Feelings** that assume the experience of either pleasure, pain, or neutrality.

- **Discrimination** has the function of comprehending the uncommon signs or characteristics of an object, to distinguish the given object from other phenomena.

- **Intention** directs the activity of each of the other factors within the primary mind with respect to the object.

- **Contact** gives rise to the changes in the senses for the three kinds of feelings through coming into contact with the object, sense power and consciousness.

- **Attention** that directs the mind to the particular object of observation.

- **Harmlessness** enables the mind to refrain from physical, verbal, and mental harmful actions. This is of the nature of compassion.

The first five are omnipresent mental factors that accompany every primary mind. These five mental factors are neutral, and the 'harmlessness' mental factor is one of the 11 virtuous mental factors. Altogether, there are 51 mental factors, according to Buddhist texts.

Mental sense power (or the sixth sense power)

The six sense powers are eyes, ears, nose, tongue, body, and mental sense powers. The first five sense powers are associated with the physical body. The sixth sense power—the 'mental sense power'—is associated with the mind. The objects that appear to the first five sense powers are respectively visual form, sound, odour, taste, and touch. The objects that appear to the mental sense power are mental objects or phenomena, such as the image of a Buddha visualised during meditation. Each of the six sense powers has its unique objects of sensing. For example, what can be sensed by the eyes (shapes and colours) can't be sensed by the ears.

In relation to each sense power, there is a corresponding 'sense consciousness'. There are, therefore, six sense consciousnesses: eye, ear, nose, tongue, body, and mental (or the sixth) sense consciousness. These sense consciousnesses take hold of the objects sensed by the sense powers in the form of mental objects and send them to the mental—or sixth—consciousness for processing — recording, filing, comparing, and analysing.

Meritorious

Virtuous intentions and paths of action are referred to as being 'meritorious' because they generate merits for the actor.

Merits

The good fortune accumulated through virtuous actions. The fulfilment of efforts in attaining material wealth, good health, long life, mental concentration, spiritual stability, pure moral conduct, realisation of wisdom, etc., depends on the specific merits accumulated.

The three key elements in generating supreme and immeasurable merits are, first and foremost, **altruistic motivation**, followed by **actions that benefit all sentient beings**, and completed by the **dedication of the merits** created to the enlightenment of all sentient beings immediately after the virtuous actions are accomplished.

Omniscience

This refers to the capacity of a fully enlightened mind that knows everything. Only a fully enlightened Buddha has an unobstructed view of reality, is unlimited by time and space, and can see the specific causes and conditions of all phenomena.

Sentient beings

Sentient beings are beings who are alive and who have consciousness and feelings. Relative to the enlightened state of a Buddha, sentient beings are ignorant of the true nature of existence and therefore commit negative karma — mental, verbal, and physical actions based on wrong information and thus leading to suffering. Buddhas and their offspring (Bodhisattvas), on the other hand, only act out of great compassion for all sentient beings due to their correct view of reality.

Shakyamuni Buddha

Shakyamuni Buddha is the Buddha of our world and time. This is established in the sense that Shakyamuni Buddha attained full enlightenment about 2500 years ago in India, and his teachings are still being practised in the world today.

The Three Jewels of *Buddha, Dharma,* and *Sangha*

Dharma refers to the wisdom, paths, and practices that lead to the true happiness of full enlightenment. Buddha is the teacher who demonstrates the *Dharma* out of great compassion for all sentient beings. *Sangha* is the name given to Buddha's advanced disciples, who have attained direct perception of the true nature of existence.

To experience true happiness and be free from all suffering, one needs to attain the realisation of the true nature of existence, as taught by Buddha. Such realisation can be attained with the help of the *Sangha*, who have experienced such attainments through their practice of the *Dharma*. Because *Buddha*, *Dharma* and *Sangha* offer refuge for sentient beings seeking happiness, they are named 'the Three Jewels'.

Vajra

A *vajra* is a thunderbolt, often with five spokes: one in the centre and one in each of the cardinal directions. It is a symbol of mental stability that is immovable or unshakable. Such immovable conviction in the mind is established by seeing the truth through both intellectual analysis and direct experience.

Very subtle mind

This refers to the state of mind that is free from any mental formations, or the mind in its natural state, or the state of mind beyond thoughts, feelings, and consciousness.

When a sentient being is born into a body, a seed of this natural state of mind is preserved in the heart centre of the central channel. The seed is called the 'indestructible drop'. This mind manifests briefly when the mind leaves the body at death. At this point, the being experiences the 'clear light mind' that can perceive the true nature of existence. However, only the mind trained to recognise clear light mind can recognise it and thus benefit from the experience.

Virtuous/Non-virtuous actions

Thoughts, speech and bodily actions performed under the influence of compassionate intention and other virtuous mental factors are virtuous. The effects of such actions are that the sentient being performing them will enjoy happiness in the future.

Actions done under the influence of ignorance, attachment, and hatred are non-virtuous. The effects of non-virtuous actions are that the performer will experience suffering in the future.

Wind energy

Energy is inseparably associated with every single thought or feeling. In other words, it takes energy to think or feel. 'Wind energy' is associated with changes in mental activities such as thoughts and feelings. At a more profound level, the mind itself is simultaneously cognition and brightness, meaning the mind itself has the intelligence and energy to form a mental object, as well as to determine what the object is. The 'wind' is the movement or change of mental energy as the mental formation and the cognition of the mental formation change.

APPENDIX

References

Aryadeva, *Four Hundred Stanzas on the Middle Way*.

His Holiness, the XIV Dalai Lama, *Activating Bodhichitta and a Meditation on Compassion*.

His Holiness, the XIV Dalai Lama, *Stages of Meditation: training the mind for wisdom*; (Commentary on Kamalashila's *The Stages of Meditation*).

Lama Tsong Khapa, *The Great Treatise on the Stages of the Path to Enlightenment*.

Lama Tsong Khapa, *The Three Principal Aspects of the Path*.

Lati Rinbochay and Elizabeth Napper, *Mind in Tibetan Buddhism*.

Nagarjuna, *Mulamadhyamakakarika*.

Shantideva, *A Guide to the Bodhisattva's Way of Life*.

Compassion Mantra

ཨོཾ་མ་ཎི་པདྨེ་ཧཱུྃ།

OM MANI PEME HUM

Great Compassion Mantra

ན་མོ་རཏྣ་ཏྲ་ཡཱ་ཡ།

ན་མཿ ཨཱརྱ་ཛྙཱ་ན་སཱ་ག་ར།

བཻ་རོ་ཙ་ན་བྱུ་ཧ་ར་ཛཱ་ཡ།

ཏ་ཐཱ་ག་ཏཱ་ཡ།

ཨརྷ་ཏེ་སམྱཀྶཾ་བུདྡྷ་ཡ། ན་མཿ

སརྦ་ཏ་ཐཱ་ག་ཏེ་བྷྱཿ ཨརྷད་བྷྱཿ

སམྱཀྶཾ་བུདྡྷེ་བྷྱཿ ན་མཿ

ཨཱརྱ་ཨ་ཝ་ལོ་ཀི་ཏེ་ཤྭ་རཱ་ཡ།

བོ་དྷི་སཏྭ་ཡ། མཧཱ་སཏྭ་ཡ།

མཧཱ་ཀཱ་རུ་ཎི་ཀཱ་ཡ། ཏདྱ་ཐཱ།

ཨོཾ་དྷ་ར་དྷ་ར། དྷི་རི་དྷི་རི།

དྷུ་རུ་དྷུ་རུ། ཨི་ཊྚེ། ཝི་ཊྚེ།

ཙ་ལེ་ཙ་ལེ། པྲ་ཙ་ལེ་པྲ་ཙ་ལེ།

ཀུ་སུ་མེ། ཀུ་སུ་མེ།

ཝ་རེ་ཨི་ལི་མི་ལི།

ཙི་ཏི་ཛྭ་ལཾ་ཨཱ་པ་ན་ཡེ་སྭཱ་ཧཱ།

NAMO RATNA TRA YA YA/ NAMA ARYA JANA SAGARA/ VAIROCHANA VYUHA RAJAYA/ TATHAGATAYA/ ARHATE SAMYAK SAM BUDDHAYA/ NAMA SARVA TATHAGATE BAYE ARHATE BAYE/ SAMYAK SAM BUDDHE BAYE/ NAMO ARYA AVALOKITE SHORAYA/ BODHI SATTVAYA/ MAHA SATTVAYA MAHA KARUNI KAYA/ TEYATHA/ OM DHARA DHARA/ DHIRI DHIRI/ DHURU DHURU/ ITTE VATTE/ CHALE CHALE/ TRACHALE TRACHALE/ KUSUME KUSUME VARE/ ILI MILI/ CHITI DZOLA MAPANAYE SVAHA

To access an audio recording of either the Compassion Mantra or the Great Compassion Mantra, focus your phone camera at the QR code below and follow the prompts.

Compassion Mantra *Great Compassion Mantra*

ABOUT LAMA TENDAR

Lama Tendar has been a Tibetan Buddhist monk since the age of 12. He received authentic teachings in the sacred practice of the Highest Yoga Tantra from his masters, who are part of an unbroken lineage of the *Dharma*. Lama Tendar studied at Gyuto Ramoche Monastery in Lhasa for eight years, where he trained with his teacher, an authentic Tibetan Medicine Healer. Lama Tendar then studied further in Gyuto Monastery in India for 16 years, where he became a qualified teacher in Mahayana Buddhism.

Lama Tendar is the founder of the Medicine Buddha Tantrayana Meditation Centre (*medicinebuddhacentre.net*) and Shantideva Buddhist Foundation. Since he moved to Melbourne in the early 2000s, he has been travelling throughout Australia, teaching Buddhist *Dharma* and providing healing for many individuals and community groups. He lives his life to benefit all sentient beings through the practice of wisdom and compassion.

ABOUT ANI DECHEN

Ani Dechen has a PhD in Economics of Development from the Australian National University and has worked as an academic for over 25 years. In seeking spiritual wellbeing, Ani Dechen learned Reiki healing with Martine Salerno from 2005 to 2006. Since 2007, she has been studying Buddhism under the guidance of Lama Tendar. While taking care of her father, who passed away in 2011, she discovered the power of Buddhist practice as a reliable source of spiritual care for people going through life-death circling. In 2014, she started to work professionally as a natural healing therapist. In searching for answers to mental and physical health issues for her clients, Ani Dechen discovered Buddhism to be a treasure trove for the science of living a fulfilling life. In 2017, she became an ordained Buddhist nun in the lineage of the Tibetan Buddhist tradition. This began her quest for mental transformation for the benefit of all sentient beings. She is very grateful to all her spiritual teachers for their compassionate guidance, care, and generous wisdom teachings.

For more information on this or any
Blue Gaia World Publishers® release,
please visit our website:

www.bluegaiapublishing.com